Maturing as a Mystic

Del Hungerford

Available from www.amazon.com, www.healingfrequenciesmusic.com, and other retail outlets where applicable.

ISBN: 978-1-7340956-2-3

Healing Frequencies Music Publications
Oldtown, ID 83822
USA

Special thanks to:
Dick Rabil for cover design
KingdomCovers.com for formatting
Lisa Thompson for editing

Contents

*I say that every word in this book is
cloaked in God's unconditional
love, peace, and joy.
I release truth and wisdom
over you as you join me on my
mystical spiritual journey
through Kingdom School.
May you come to full maturity
as a Christ-companion through
developing a deeper relationship
with your one, true, Creator.*

Introduction

THIS BOOK WAS birthed in the summer of 2019 as I had a conversation with God about life's trials and how they mature us. The information from that discussion sat for over two years until one day, God said it was time to revisit it. The main idea for the content compares grade school, middle school, and college with spiritual schooling that I call "Kingdom School." It's a process of maturing in a grade-like manner that includes tests in the form of life trials and daily living.

The title of this book reflects my mystical journey into understanding the mysteries of our Creator. Although I came out of a Christian-based mindset, not everyone on a mystical journey comes from a similar background. What we call the Divine Creator doesn't really matter. Our connection with the unconditional love of God doesn't require that we use the same name. I use "God" because it's familiar to most people.

Our Creator is not a respecter of persons, so it doesn't matter whether you're an agnostic, Catholic, charismatic, Muslim, etc. God's love for us is not determined by which religion we choose. My approach is based on my Christian background because that's what I experienced. This includes the use of Scripture. For those who come from other cultures, you will find that writings in many sacred texts mirror what's in the Bible. May you receive from my words what rings true in your spirit.

God speaks to us through an approach that we understand. For me, it's school related topics, my Christian walk, nature, and music. As in my previous books, I see myself sitting with members of the Trinity (Father, Son, and Holy Spirit) and the cloud of witnesses (those who have died and gone before us) in heavenly places during our conversations. I'm in my physical body writing while my spirit is "ascended" and in communion with the Trinity. I call this the "in him" principle because I picture using the "eyes of my heart" (my imagination) in Christ, looking through His eyes.

"Ascension" is a current buzzword for living fulltime in the presence of God. It's based on supernatural experiences and encounters with the Trinity where we administrate our life in the spiritual realm first, then release that revelation into our natural surroundings. We do this through the "In him" principle as we see ourselves one with Christ where "living life" occurs from this position. We function like Enoch, Ezekiel, Elijah, Daniel, Jesus, Moses, and others in the Bible who walked daily with God. Supernatural occurrences came through their relationship with the Trinity.

I find it fascinating that my heavenly encounters closely mirror near death experiences. I'm amazed at how these stories line up with what I experience daily. What people often see on their death bed confirms that my encounters with the Trinity aren't anything I'm making up. My ascension experiences are as real as the words you're reading on this page. The main ingredient with true heavenly encounters is the unconditional love of God. When people marinate in this type of love, they are changed forever because nothing else compares to pure love that comes directly from the heart of God.

When it was time to choose the stories that are included in this writing, I heard, "Use those from the eminent domain situation." I'll be honest, after reading the encounters for the first time in over two years, I was ashamed of my responses. My childish behavior made me cringe – for a moment. If I can't be honest enough to share my failures as well as successes, I'm not being true to myself. Why would I not want to share those stories as well? I've learned more from my failures than successes. Losing my home through the process of eminent domain was the icing-on-the-cake of trials that included a mixture of failures and successes.

We often get stuck in a revolving door of circumstances, unable to find the exit when our belief is that leaders, prophets, and teachers know best. We don't learn to exercise our own spiritual senses, which is how we get stuck in a revolving door. We can get lazy, complacent, and too busy to "search out a thing." Eventually, we become programmed to think and act a certain way. If we want to find the exit, it requires a willingness to let go of everything we've ever been taught and believed.

I eventually exited the revolving door, but not without challenges. If we're willing to put everything aside that we know about God, the journey into His deeper mysteries begins. Along the way, we may wonder "Is that God or the pizza I ate last night talking to me?" As we step into our Creator's eyes through the "in him" principle, we directly interact with "His ways." What comes from these encounters may be extremely shocking. God presented differing perspectives of Biblical principles to me. What He said was often opposite of what I'd learned from people I deemed wiser than myself.

I chose to step out of religious thinking, including all the required rules. When rules become a "god," we're enslaved to them. If rules and regulations dictate our relationship with God, then our relationship is with the rules, not a divine Creator. Our "savior" becomes the rules and regulations.

To let go of the milk of the Word and start eating meat, Hebrews 5:12-14 says we must learn and experience God's truths for ourselves. Teachers, leaders, and parents mentor and feed us when we're babies. "Graduating" from milk to meat requires action on our part where we become responsible for our personal well-being. Until we make the decision to do that, we're "babies" in the things of God, even if we know the Bible inside and out. Eating the meat of the word requires action – actions that lead to results.

When I first started the ascension journey, I didn't know anyone else doing it. If I wanted to learn the principles of kingdom living, I wasn't going to wait for others to lead the way. I look back on the changes in my life and know I'm in the best position I've ever been. I'm less stressed out, I function with a more restful state of mind, and I'm learning how to live from a position of unconditional love. How do I know it's working? When I respond more out of love than fear despite what goes on around me, I've made progress. When my conduct lines up with God's character, I'm living by what's in the Bible.

In this book, we put personal responsibility and maturity to the test. In the supporting workbook, available on Amazon, I provide ascension exercises for you to engage with. Bottom line – if we want a better relationship with God, it's going to require some action on our part. This is one reason I added a supporting workbook. It's an opportunity for you to practice what I write about here. Your journey may be extremely uncomfortable at times but in the end, it's well worth it. Like me, you'll make mistakes. Who cares? Go with it as God leads you on a journey into greater maturity! Losing my home through the eminent domain process provided an opportunity for me to put my big girl pants on. How well did I do? The answer lies ahead.

Maturing as a Mystic
Del Hungerford

Maturing as a Mystic

Prelude

MAYBE BECAUSE I was saved in grade school amid tough family circumstances, I didn't internalize weird religious teachings. I wasn't mature enough to understand adult speak. I never held leadership roles in church either, which probably shielded me from additional trauma. I witnessed a lot of interesting behavior by those in leadership, which puzzled my young mind. Their conduct didn't line up with what I read in Scripture. A 1970s song called "They'll Know We Are Christians by Our Love" spoke to my heart during those early years. This song helped me internalize the need to demonstrate instead of just using my mouth.

I learned to take God at His Word and ignored the weird preaching by leadership. In my world, if words and actions don't match, I tend to put my attention elsewhere. I learned that life events (the good, the bad, and the ugly) are necessary parts of our journey. When a circumstance rears its ugly head, I ask, "What can I learn *from* this?" I focus on understanding the lesson so that I can graduate to the next level in life. Answers might elude me, but the fact that God *is* love and is not a respecter of persons (2 Peter 3:9) brings me to a new level of maturity somehow. It's all about walking in faith and trusting that if God is who he says he is, I'll make it to the other side. When the Bible says that God loves everyone, I believe it means *everyone*. If God plays favorites, then 2 Peter 3:9 is a lie. We are created in *his* image, and we're called his children, so we can be like him.

Even before I started high school, I purposed that I would use life situations as tools in my own Christian walk. Because people function out of a sinful nature, we don't always get it right. The more we learn to function in Christ, the easier it is to operate from peace and rest despite what is going on around us.

In college, I joined a fellowship with a husband-wife team as co-leaders. They were graduates of Rhema Bible School under the tutelage of Kenneth Hagin. Pastor Marvin was a Messianic Jew and former chiropractor. After a long career as a doctor, he felt called into the ministry. Marvin and Pam's lives emulated what I'd read in the Bible about God's character; they lived what they preached. There was no secret sin. Finally, what I'd understood about God's love and character as a child, I witnessed in action through my leaders. This gave me hope that my understanding of God's Word wasn't wonky.

My growing-up years were difficult and odd at times. Eventually, an abusive marriage nearly took my life. I write about that in my first book, *But Words Will Never Hurt Me*. During this very low time, I allowed circumstances to get the better of me. I lost track of the "God is love" principle and functioned out of my own pain. That didn't work too well for me. It took fifteen years after the marriage ended to recover emotionally and physically from living the lies that I'd come into agreement with.

Here, I share how losing my home to eminent domain matured me even further. Trouble in River City is not always a negative thing. I had a lot to learn about my own selfish desires, in addition to understanding the bigger picture. What? You mean losing your home to a highway can be a positive thing? Of course, it all depends on how we view a situation. I had to learn that God was *in* this move! Walking through the eminent domain process provided an opportunity to be schooled in the more mature things of the kingdom. It was my invitation to enroll in kingdom college.

In this book, I introduce the concept of kingdom school, where we look at life and maturity in Christ as moving from one grade level to the next. In the supporting workbook, I provide the activations I used on my journey. We tend to mature in a somewhat progressive manner where we have opportunities along the way that test our ability to function at any given level. It's no big deal if we fail because, in God, we always get do-overs. No two people are the same, so kingdom school will look different for each of us.

For years, I was a band director in public schools. I used a teaching method a group of us developed called Band Olympics. Students colored *Far Side* characters and raced them over "hurdles" posted around the band room. To get over a hurdle, students had to demonstrate certain musical principles. The semester grade was based on how many hurdles they completed. Students could try a level as many times as needed until they could get over that hurdle. By the middle of the school year, creatively colored *Far Side* characters littered the walls of my band room.

I see kingdom school like I taught Band Olympics. The Trinity is our guide along with the cloud of witnesses (those who've died and are now in heaven to coach us) and our assigned angels. We learn by engaging with God's Word, having conversations with him, watching what he does, and by following his example. It's completely up to us to get over life's hurdles so we can advance toward the next test. In a sense, we go from maturity to maturity. What stops us from advancing to the next hurdle? Here's an introductory list with my suggested grade levels:

- The biggest issue starts with an inability to understand our identity in Christ. We are in him, and he's in us. We can do *all* things through Christ who strengthens us. (See Philippians 4:13.) This is taught in kingdom grade school and hopefully put into full practice by kingdom high school.
- We allow past failures to keep us from moving forward. When we do that, we're responding out of fear. Fear always keeps us stationary. When we're operating out of fear, we take a trip back to kingdom grade school.
- We often live out of life's traumas, which causes a victim mentality. A victim mentality indicates this subject is at a kingdom grade school level.
- Our society likes to focus too much on the aches and pains of our physical bodies. The same is true with our emotional state. This

encourages our soul to rule instead of our spirit. Anything negative is at the kingdom grade school level.

- Because society tends to veer toward a pessimistic bent in life, we often see the glass as half-empty rather than half-full. This is a lifestyle of negative thinking. Negativity and fear lower our immune systems, which then opens us up to sickness and disease. Again, this subject is at the kingdom grade school level.
- As Christians, we tend not to understand the fullness of our true authority in Christ. As we step into the kingdom middle and high school levels, we begin to understand our authority at a higher comprehension level.
- We forget that the words of our mouth create life and death. (See Proverbs 18:21.) Until we reign in our thoughts, we will see the effects of this at all levels.
- We tend to focus on what is the opposite of God's solution. This is taught in kingdom grade school as standard operating procedure because we're still shifting into seeing things as God sees them.
- We don't have to wait until we die to go to heaven. This is about developing a deeper relationship with the Trinity beyond the stories and truths we read in the Bible. This is part of kingdom college lessons. However, we can see snippets of it at earlier levels.
- Our focus is often on the things of the world over relationship with the Trinity. This is standard operating procedure in kingdom grade school because we're still practicing the principle of dwelling in him.
- We now live in a microwave society where we desire immediate results, so many of us struggle with discipline and consistent follow-through. This is a grade school mindset. As we mature into the upper grades, we learn to understand God's timing.
- We tend to give up too easily when we don't see positive results as quickly as we'd like. This is a typical grade school mindset. At the middle school level, we begin to understand that persistence is necessary.

Through my journey in kingdom school, I take you back in time as I lose my home through eminent domain. My hope is that key points of my experience will resonate with you and assist you on your own journey. We often walk through unnerving life lessons. We honestly need to learn to be uncomfortable. Why? Without challenges in life, we become complacent, which can lead to a lack of forward motion, lower levels of maturity, and minimal character building.

CHAPTER 1

Kingdom Grades 1-2

GRADE SCHOOL KIDS are extremely self-focused. Everything is about "me, me, me" and what I need. They generally do not have enough maturity to understand the needs and desires of others unless their parents focus on these matters. Even then, a grade school student needs to be reminded to think about others. At this stage of development, they are still discovering who they are, what they're capable of, and how to channel their energy.

In kingdom school, I liken immature Christians to grade school students because we tend to function out of life experiences, allowing these to define who we are. We're discovering our identity in Christ while flip-flopping between understanding spiritual principles with what we see in the natural as our reality. We are more focused on living life here on earth because tuning into spiritual awareness is in the developmental stages. If we had spiritual experiences as children, those memories can be wiped away because adults say things such as, "It's only your imagination." In a sense, we stuff anything that doesn't line up with reason.

Everything is determined by the effort we put into it. At times, we're in three or four levels at the same time in different subjects, such as godly character, emotional state, understanding biblical principles, consistency, living in or from life traumas, attitudes, and paradigms. As you'll see in a couple of my stories, I crisscross over several grade levels in a span of a few moments.

Grade 1:

First graders have amazing imaginations, and through play, they discover life. It's a time of imaginary friends, play-acting, and self-discovery. I know very few children at this age who do not have a vivid imagination. The key here is the word "imagination." It's a gift from God, so don't be afraid of it!

Our imaginations are an integral part of our core being: spirt, soul, and body. The ability to imagine is what leads to inventions, amazing ideas, and all forms of creativity that can become life careers. It's appropriate that a baby Christ follower begins as a kingdom first grader. By faith, sanctify your imagination, asking God to help you judge what's from him and what isn't.

Spiritual first grade is when a person decides to live a Christ-like life. Like someone beginning to read, they need assistance from others who have practiced living biblical truths. Mentors show the way by example. I say "mentor" because it doesn't have to be someone in leadership. Mentors are those more mature than we are. They offer assistance that points in the general direction with options for individual needs. The student must practice repeatedly, like a child learning to write letters in the alphabet. Mentorship can also be through teachings, conferences, on-line classes, gatherings of like-minded people, etc.

This is where we're introduced to the truths in the Bible but don't yet understand or have the discipline to walk out the relationship of practicing godly concepts. We discover through experience along with studying truths in God's Word. We also absorb information about love, faith, hope, peace, etc., and how they work in real-life situations. We then apply these truths to our individual circumstances.

Self-starters and others learn to come before God, seeking him directly. We see this when people have had visitations from God and often don't even know his name. They don't have access to Bibles, so the only way they learn is through experience. We hear stories about this phenomenon coming out of China, Africa, and other unchurched countries.

The early church didn't have the Bible, so how do you suppose they learned the ways of God? They had letters from Paul and others that eventually made it into the Bible. These writers developed a personal relationship with God without the Bible. They learned to walk beside him daily, discovering his ways through what I call the "come up here" principle described in Revelation 4:1. Since we do have access to Bibles, one way of engaging with God is to step into a story, asking the Trinity to take us there.

Grade 2:

Second graders, like first graders, are very creative with amazing imaginations. They are finding themselves as a human through a discovery process. They make lots of mistakes while they learn to focus. Seasoned teachers encourage children during the mistake-making process, so students aren't fearful of moving forward. Attention spans of young elementary students are very short, so teachers must learn to vary activities that enhance a diverse learning experience. Young elementary students need lots of modeling so they have something to mimic. Students at this age don't yet have a high level of comprehension. They learn by watching and copying.

In spiritual second grade, we practice even more and are given larger chunks of material to learn. At this grade level, people are still considered baby Christ followers because they need lots of examples. During this stage, some leaders begin to exert control, often leading the babes to follow their own guidelines for behavior and maturity. There's lots of experimenting like a two-year-old with a new toy. We may not use our tools correctly, but we sure have fun while we see what they can do. Experimentation helps with critical thinking skills.

We begin to realize our circumstances caused trauma and pain that need healing and restoration. We may or may not yet comprehend these issues can hold us back. That's because we've practiced negative behaviors for so long, we don't realize they are wrapped up in trauma. What I do to help alleviate this problem is ask God to show me right away when something causes a negative trigger. Negative triggers are almost always indicative that something needs healing. According to scientific evidence, physical issues have emotional roots.[1]

---

1   Amanda MacMillan, "Why Mental Illness Can Fuel Physical Disease," *Time*, February 23, 2017, https://time.com/4679492/depression-anxiety-chronic-disease.

When people sign up for the Healing Frequencies Music newsletter,[2] they get a chart in one of the emails that compares illnesses with various emotional roots. In this way, I can help people identify possible causes of what may hold them back from advancing to a new level of maturity. The key at this level is to begin identifying which life situations may hold us back from further levels of maturity.

---

2   www.healingfrequenciesmusic.com

CHAPTER 2:

Kingdom Grades 3-6

GRADE 3:

I call this level the comprehension stage. A typical third grader begins to understand more about choices and the consequences that come with their decisions. As a music teacher, I couldn't get first and second graders to do anything on their own. By third grade, creative juices flow much better. I could tell students, "Make up your own rhythm," and they'd do it. In first and second grade, I demonstrated the activity, and they copied what I did. But younger students gave me the deer-in-the-headlights look when I asked them to be creative on their own. Some could. Those who couldn't copied other students.

In kingdom third grade, we gain the ability to understand biblical truths and learn more about God's character. We begin doing things on our own without feeling the need to check in with institutional leadership. We learn more about our identity as a child of God. We should be free to step out, experiment, and make mistakes. Why is that? We learn best from our bloopers.

Those who only do what leadership instructs rarely get past grade three in kingdom school. Let me reiterate that point—when we only do what we're taught and aren't encouraged to explore on our own, we can get stuck at this grade level. One must be able to use critical thinking skills to pass kingdom third grade. We must question godly truths and experience what's in the Bible so we have personal revelation that takes us further than what we're hearing from those we are told know more than we do. If we have to follow a lot of rules, we probably won't move past kingdom third grade until we can break away from that legalism.

How do we know if we're stuck at this level? I pose a question followed by a possible answer. Notice they all involve a follow-up action. If any of these ring true, consider seeking inner healing to help bring you back to a creative and imaginative place in your being.

- Do you go home after hearing what you've been taught, knowing it to be true, and regularly put it into practice? If you answer no, this may indicate a need for more personal discipline, experimentation, and searching out truths.
- Do you take a teacher's word as truth without further research or your own experience? If you answer yes, this may indicate a need to do your own studying, asking God to show you his truth in what was taught. This also requires personal discipline.
- Do leaders indicate how much you're to tithe, how you're to act, how you're to dress, and how you're to behave? Have leaders made themselves gods over you? If you answer yes, this may indicate you need to assess why you feel the need to answer to someone in place of God.
- Have you been taught that you must perform, do, or be a certain way to receive God's love and acceptance? If you answer yes, this may indicate you need a paradigm shift about the truth of God's love.
- Have you been taught that God is an angry God who demands complete obedience to be loved? If you answer yes, this may suggest a needed paradigm shift in understanding that God is loving and doesn't require anything of you but to be yourself. *Nothing* you do will make him love you any more or less.

- Have you been taught and then followed specific rules and regulations that will advance you into greater favor with God? If you answer yes, this may indicate a need to work through the trauma of these teachings via inner healing along with asking God to teach you more about the power of his love.
- Do you feel spiritually abused by previous leaders? If you answer, this may indicate a need for inner healing to work through the trauma of the experience.

GRADE 4:

Before going deeper into level four, please understand that it's possible to flip-flop back and forth across grade levels. You may only be stuck in one area while operating in a higher level in other areas. For example, I was emotionally stunted after living through an abusive marriage. I had sound biblical teaching but wasn't living it during the marriage because I let circumstances—not God's answer—rule me. Therefore, I reverted to living at a middle school level emotionally, which required that I get some inner healing.

Fourth graders begin to be a bit more aware of what others think of them. They're not yet at the socially awkward stage where they're embarrassed at their behaviors. Fourth grade seems to be a transition age, right before puberty. They are still imaginative and can do more without being prompted. Comprehension leaps forward for most fourth graders.

Spiritually speaking, grade four involves taking what we understand in the first three levels and making it part of our daily lives. We are learning that we can practice God's presence as our go-to method of functioning. Personal discipline is a requirement from this point forward. We continually work through issues that need inner healing as we understand the greater mystery of God's love for us. We learn that God wants to be part of our daily lives. We may or may not yet understand that we can have conversations with the Trinity like we do with any friend. However, we are better able to comprehend many truths outlined in the Bible. We are learning to make those truths stick in our behaviors. This age still focuses a lot on personal needs and desires.

We are developing personal character but probably need lots of practice before it's cemented into our natural behavior. Character is practiced—it's not a gift. We are given many opportunities in life's tests to advance our character. In my marriage, I failed this test quite miserably. Triggers brought out many negative characteristics. Eventually, I shut down completely as a coping mechanism. My character building took a hit, but once I got back on track, the maturity growth picked up quickly because of my growth prior to the marriage. This is an example of going back and forth across maturity levels based on life circumstances. It's okay to do this. If we don't learn from life's trials, we don't have the needed experiences for maturity to stay at higher levels in future situations.

GRADE 5:

By fifth grade, puberty is starting to kick in for most children. This is when they become very self-aware of their bodies and what they can do to be accepted. They have a higher level of comprehension and retention. Trained specialists in specific academic areas assist them with the learning process. Students are growing up emotionally, physically, and educationally.

Spiritually, by this stage, we shouldn't expect others to do *for us*. We have more responsibility for our actions because we have a greater understanding of what we're doing. We know we will face a possible negative outcome if we choose to do something a certain way. We quit conference hopping, going from one place to the next, hoping for the next greatest move of God. We don't need a spiritual fix to get us from one week to the next because we understand that a personal relationship with God is an important part of daily life. If we come home from a conference and feel let down, we put into practice what we experienced. What we gain at these events should assist our maturity and character-building process. Our best times of intimacy and closeness to God are when no one else is around and God has our individual and undivided attention.

As we mature, we can easily mentor others, sharing our life experiences as examples in how we've overcome obstacles along the way. By kingdom fifth grade, we understand the need to continue learning and seek out teachings and experiences that advance us into greater levels of maturity. We are well on our way to understanding that a personal relationship with God is a key driving factor and that doing is not required of us. We are learning to step into peace and rest during difficult situations.

We continue to work through issues that hold us back. We are introduced through personal study to the deeper truths in the Bible. We no longer need others to spoon feed us because we can identify and deal with the simple things that keep us from moving forward. At this stage, we deal with deeper levels of trauma because we have a greater level of comprehension into hurtful life issues that stunted our growth.

GRADE 6:

When fifth graders return for sixth grade, they are totally different. It's like having mini-grown-ups in class. The girls begin to look like women. Many of the boys' voices have lowered, and suddenly, they're interested in the opposite sex. Until this age, many students are rarely embarrassed, but once they hit sixth grade, wowzer!

I had one young man who was a third grader when I started teaching at his school. He did some of the goofiest things for attention. One day in sixth grade, he was playing finger games with a new girl in the school. I stopped teaching to watch for a moment, trying to figure out what they were doing. The rest of the class did the same. When he noticed we were all watching, he was extremely embarrassed. This was a huge change for a kid who, three months earlier, relished in the thrill of making bodily noises so he could watch the reaction of his classmates.

In our walk with the Trinity, sixth-grade kingdom school is very similar. We've gone through our goofy, sporadic, and undisciplined behaviors where we realize through maturity that some behaviors we previously engaged in could now cause issues. We are more aware of others, what they're thinking, and how we can connect with them.

We are at our first graduation level. Six is the number of man, which indicates that it's in our best interest to graduate from acting in the flesh to functioning from the spirit. We understand that spiritual gifts are practiced and fine-tuned. We are on our way to understanding our identity in Christ, although here, it's still at an elementary level. Because we continually work on life's traumas, we may still struggle with understanding that "in him we live, move, and have our being" (Acts 17:28). This is a great spiritual truth where we realize that as we step into our position in Christ, we don't need to function out of past trauma and experiences that can keep us from truly understanding who we are. We still look to teachings and revelation from others at a similar or greater maturity level than we are.

Chapter Conclusion:

After watching the Christian community for the better part of my life, many often do not appear to be aware of what stunts growth. What occurred in childhood, previous relationships, life traumas, spiritual abuse from leadership, or a myriad of other situations garners the blame. I frequently hear these types of statements: "This happened when I was a child so, I can't _____." The blame tends to be aimed at the situation or at others involved.

I'll use myself as an example of how this works. After leaving the abusive marriage, one of my friends consistently said that I had a part to play. Honestly, it made me mad. I curtly said to her, "I didn't ask him to abuse me!" Her response generally went something like, "You didn't have to stay in the relationship." Thank God for friends who can help us even when they have to say hard things.

For quite some time, I didn't understand what my friend meant. Then, one day, several years later, I was having a conversation with Jesus about something totally unrelated to my marriage. Our discussion focused on attitudes and where we get stuck in moving forward. He asked me a question, which I couldn't answer. I realized the conversation was leading to my attitude about my part in the abusive marriage. After Jesus asked more questions that prompted additional thinking and pondering, the light came on in my brain. I looked at Jesus and said, "It's because I believed the lies my husband threw at me!"

With a smile, he replied, "Bingo!"

At first, I was stymied when I realized one simple wrong paradigm held me back in an area of discovery concerning a current situation. Once that roadblock was removed, it didn't take long for me to move past the point where I was stuck. The moment I realized what I'd done, right before Jesus, I admitted it. "I own the belief system of functioning out of my husband's lies. I renounce all ties to that belief system, and I repent for my behavior. I nail these attitudes to the cross where they're crucified. I then walk them through the cross where they are covered by the blood of Jesus, and I trade them for more of Your love." (These weren't my exact words but communicate the message.)

I've learned to immediately take care of problems once I realize there's an issue. I don't argue. Matthew 5:25 says to quickly agree with your adversary. I repent even when I think I've done no wrong. If I didn't do it, someone in my generational line probably did, and by repenting, I'm releasing that person as well. The goal is to be free from guilt, anger, unforgiveness, and other negative character traits as we become more like Christ. Why do we want wrong paradigms if they're going to hold us back, keeping us from living life to the fullest in Christ?

The goal by the end of kingdom middle school is to move from physical, soulish, and emotional living into higher spiritual awareness and mode of functioning from the spirit. That can't happen if we hold on to unforgiveness, fear, and anger; allow life traumas or frustrations to negatively affect us; and live out of our past instead of the future. As we mature, our reactions aren't ruled as much by our emotions. We function by living through the in-him principle where we're at peace despite what goes on around us. We're led more and more by the Spirit, and when bad situations occur, they don't negatively affect our psyche. The good news? If we're moving forward, even an inch at a time, it's progress! It takes a lifetime to make our messes, so we can't expect an instant paradigm shift or the ability to develop new habits quickly. Everything takes practice, which takes patience and perseverance.

CHAPTER 3:

Kingdom Middle School and High School

Middle School: Grades 7 and 8

Middle school students are quite squirrely and at the rebellious stage where they buck the authority of parents and teachers. Many teachers dislike instructing this age group because of their moodiness and stubbornness as they go through puberty, learning to understand that "adulting" doesn't make sense. Each semester, I ask college music students the question, "How many of you want to teach middle school music?" That question is usually met with rolling eyes amid a variety of interesting responses. They generally agree that working with middle school students is a challenge.

Middle school students begin to focus a bit more on their appearance and what they can do to win others over, especially members of the opposite sex. In kingdom middle school, maturing Christians can act similarly: moody, emotionally unstable, and undisciplined. They want to please others and can go to great lengths to prove to leadership that they're worthy of their attention. Examples of this include wanting to be at the front of the prayer line every

Sunday, frequently looking for a personal prophetic word, signing up for many church and other activities, etc. Yeah, I did all of these, so I get it. But we should relish this great growing season. Without it, we would struggle to transition from childhood to adulthood.

Kingdom middle school is a season of learning to be accountable for our actions. This involves following through by choosing an action that matches our words. If we agree to do something, then we need to do it in a timely manner. If we can't do it, we should be responsible and let others know of the change. Failing to say anything because we're embarrassed isn't helpful. We also learn to function with integrity during this life transition.

Puberty isn't a fun time for most middle school students because they go through frustrating physical and emotional changes and seem to think one way one moment and exactly the opposite way the next. They are more reluctant to step out into unknown territory because they are so self-aware.

Spiritually speaking, Kingdom middle school is a great place to be. Students have the opportunity to do much more experimenting and learn to do things on their own instead of following the "I teach—you regurgitate back to me" mentality. We get to practice putting on our "big girl (or boy) Christian pants." Christian puberty involves a decision to walk away from childish ways so we can eat the meat of the Word. (1 Corinthians 13:11; Hebrews 5:12–14) Parents or older siblings prepare meals for children. Mature people can cook and prepare their own meals. Although I started cooking when I was nine, I needed to follow a recipe. By the time I reached high school, I was more adept at throwing a meal together without a recipe because I now understood what combinations of food worked together and how much of each ingredient was needed. Christian maturity from milk to meat is very similar. Young Christians need help, and mature Christians can do life in Christ with minimal assistance. Mature Christians can handle it when their peers in Christ need to correct them as you saw with my friend earlier who said I had a responsibility for the abuse in my marriage.

The level of growth expected from eighth to ninth grade requires a huge leap. High school offers extra-curricular activities in abundance, and there's pressure to do as much as possible to prepare for college. Colleges not only look at grades but at how many extracurricular activities a student can squeeze in while keeping their grades up. High school is all about preparing for "adulting." What will we be when we grow up? By twelfth grade, students are expected to choose a career path as they have already had enough experience in life to make that decision.

Introducing Kingdom High School

By the time Christians reach kingdom high school, they're gone through Christian puberty. High schoolers have arrived. Kingdom high school offers Christians an opportunity to step fully into the truths of the Word, develop a strong character, function with integrity, and continue to address traumas and other past issues that hold them back. They begin to walk in the calling they have on their lives.

High school students are rarely supervised unless they specifically need it. Teachers present the information, then allow students to study on their own with minimal oversight. Tests show comprehension levels. The responsibility level of high school students is much greater than in any previous grade. Students are given twice as much work and are expected to retain the information with a greater level of understanding.

High school students are introduced to group projects where each member of a team provides valuable input. For Christians, this is comparable to a group that meets with no single leader. Everyone has an equal opportunity to speak at the meeting. The New Testament church (*ecclesia* or *ekklesia*) functioned like this.[3] To operate as a healthy organization, we let go of the top-down mentality. Teamwork suggests that everyone has a part, which depends on our God-given individual gifts. It's not about "we need someone to work in the nursery." Churches dictate what their needs are. Ekklesia looks at who is there and develops a team that includes everyone's strengths in the "ekklesia puzzle." We all have a part to play, and we learn it in kingdom high school.

Spiritually speaking, maturing high-school-level Christians are expected to take what's taught and show a high level of comprehension in what they're learning. This includes putting these things into practice in everyday life. If we still rely on others to provide our daily bread, we aren't at this level yet.

---

3   *The NAS New Testament Greek Lexicon*, "ekklesia," Bible Study Tools, accessed December 15, 2021, https://www.biblestudytools.com/lexicons/greek/nas/ekklesia.html.

Being a Christian at the high school level requires that we think and respond for ourselves, often challenging concepts taught from a pulpit. However, we don't necessarily do this to a preacher's face—we do our own study. We learn to take our puzzling questions directly to God, asking him to show us missed truths. We learn through experience versus swallowing everything we hear as "thus sayeth the Lord."

In kingdom high school, we go from Christ-followers to Christ-companions. If we're in him, that means we're like Christ, which requires being more than a follower.

Grade 9

Ninth graders feel like they're at the bottom of the pile. In eighth grade, they were at the top. In a sense, it's a knock-down of identity, responsibility, and maturity. Many ninth graders feel as if they're starting from scratch because nothing is the same as they previously knew. Classes are more difficult with twice as much homework, and students are required to better manage their time. The first few weeks of ninth grade are often somewhat traumatic for many high schoolers because the changes are so different from eighth grade. Everything a ninth grader ever thought about school changes once they get to high school. Kingdom high school is no different. To move ahead to the next level or maturity, they will make major paradigm adjustments concerning religious thinking in this season.

In Christian-follower land, this is another huge responsibility and maturity challenge. Everything they've ever understood about being a Christian is up for discussion. Former life issues and traumas can taunt them, hoping they'll return to those issues because of the comfort in going back to the known. The unknown is often a scary place, so they seek what's comfortable. They find out what they've previously been taught may be wrong, so they're challenged with ridding themselves of stinking thinking. When they're stuck in a religious paradigm that requires something of them to be loved by God, they can feel lost and out-of-sorts. This is where I got stuck in my marriage and functioned at this ninth-grade level emotionally until I walked through some healing.

By ninth grade, we understand basic concepts of what's in the Word. However, we function out of book knowledge versus experiencing a relationship with a loving Father. We've read and understand a book that's full of stories about who God is. Do we know him from experience beyond what the Bible says? Unless we spend time in his presence, studying the Bible is like reading memoirs of famous people. We don't know them unless we spend time with them. We can know every aspect of their lives because we know their history, but we've never met them. Therefore, we don't really know them. We only know about them. To know Jesus, we must spend time with him, learning about his desires and concerns as much as our own. It's all about equal relationship.

In ninth grade kingdom school, we work through more traumas in our lives but can still get caught up in emotional responses to life situations. We understand our identity as people but not necessarily who we are in Christ. We learn at this stage that all life experiences contribute to our identity in Christ because he put within us gifts and talents that, when used properly, propel us into the call on our lives.

At this stage, kingdom school takes another maturity leap by ramping up the come-up-here principle. We can have visions and experiences prior to becoming a Christian, but comprehension of the heavenly experience is very different. I have a friend who went to a local mall. When she walked out, she physically saw the roof of the building lift off as it opened to heaven. She heard the voice of the Lord tell her that he wanted to start a friendship with her. But she didn't have a framework for the experience, so it left her traumatized for years.

Why would this happen? God probably already knew what her response would be. However, we are still given opportunities to respond differently. We often react a certain way because what we're seeing, sensing, hearing, or feeling is totally off our grid. That was probably the case with my friend.

If we're willing to develop a relationship with the Trinity beyond the words in the Bible, in ninth grade, we reframe everything we ever thought we knew about being a Christ-follower. This often requires tearing structures down to the foundation of our learning. It's a soulishly painful process because everything we learned to this point is up for discussion, redirection, and deconstruction. If we want to stay at this level, that's fine as well. If we want more, we will need to learn to build a relationship with God in a way we've never previously experienced. If we've had previous spiritual experiences that didn't make sense, this is the time to explore the deeper meaning of those experiences.

Grades 10, 11, and 12

I'm lumping these three grades together because students often mingle in classes, especially in the elective courses, such as languages, art, theater, music, computer courses, wood shop, and auto mechanics. Due to the mixed ages in certain classes, younger students have an opportunity to glean understanding from older students.

My teaching experience was in elementary music and middle school band. However, I subbed a lot for both the high school choir and band teachers. High school students tend to think they know it all. They argue with and challenge teachers much more than middle school kids do. At the same time, they want relationship with teachers beyond "hi, how are you?" Some want to know and understand how the adults got to where they are in life. Soon, they'll have to completely take care of themselves with minimal help from parents, especially after turning eighteen. For many high school seniors, this is both an exciting and scary time.

Kingdom high school graduates function from the revelation received during the previous grades as they practice life. They know this as God's revelation and truths. Time in high school is well spent honing these truths and learning to live in and through them. Those who are serious about biblical truths and how God's love covers everything continue to deal with life's traumas, bringing themselves into a healthier state of wholeness.

As we deconstruct religious mindsets and allow the Trinity to work *with* us because we're one with them, we're ready to begin kingdom college, should we desire to do so. Some are called to function as kingdom high school graduates while others chart a course for new territories. Why is that? Some are to assist others at or below this level. The Bible refers to this as the thirty-, sixty-, and one hundred-fold. (See John 2:14; Galatians 5:22.) If you don't feel called to this, don't sweat it! Be the best you can be as a kingdom high school graduate.

CHAPTER 4

Kingdom College

I USED TO JOKE with friends that college freshmen revert to junior high attitudes and behaviors. College freshmen are squirrely, struggle with self-discipline, and don't know how to manage their lives. For the first time, they don't have parents telling them what to do and when to do it. Many have never had to pay bills, buy food, and then feed themselves. Students study a career path to find a decent-paying job in college or trade school (equivalent of kingdom college). They treat themselves by partying and enjoying life to its fullest until the wee hours of the morning. No parent yells, "Get your homework done and go to bed!" I'm not sure bedtime even exists in college. Students are either up having too much fun or writing long papers with tight deadlines. And absent-minded professors? Yes, they do exist! Absent-minded student? They learn that skill from professors.

Kingdom college is another major leap of maturity, integrity, and character building. We go through huge paradigm shifts where everything we ever knew about life and how it's lived is new to us. We've heard about but haven't encountered this phenomenon for ourselves. We are mature in book knowledge but often lack personal experience. We've had lots of religious teaching that may or may not be correct. When we get to kingdom college, we realize our previous religious teaching needs major adjustments. That can throw us into quite a tailspin if we're not open to change. Any form of spiritual abuse makes this transition difficult. It feels as if we've taken several steps backward because what we knew and about God may not be based on truth. Well, at least that's how I felt.

Kingdom college begins for a Christian when they step into the come-up-here principle described in Revelation 4:1. John was invited to go to heaven to investigate the future. Many in Scripture had similar experiences. Jesus, Enoch, Daniel, Ezekiel, and Elijah are a few who were completely aware they could live on earth while functioning in heaven at the same time. Like them, we learn to see a thing in heaven, then administrate it on earth. We see, hear, sense, and feel God's heart as we commune with him. As stated previously, we can start kingdom college while still in high school.

Not everyone is called to live from this place. Why is that? It's difficult to teach others unless they are fairly close to our own levels. This is like asking someone in the New York Philharmonic Orchestra to teach a beginner. They are used to teaching aspiring artists and professionals, not brand-new students. I see this in music education classes when teaching students how to work with beginning band students. The concept is completely foreign to most of them because they've forgotten what they went through at that age. We need people at all levels of maturity to support and mentor others based on what we've gone through ourselves.

Many are invited out of organized religion while others stay in it. Some of those in leadership can't grasp kingdom college concepts, which makes it interesting to stay in organized religion. A lack of understanding tends to lead to accusations, such as "that's demonic." "It's not of God." "You're practicing new age stuff." "You're in error." "These aren't Biblical principles," etc. The bottom line is we're to foster an intimate relationship with God. If we want the fullness of what that brings, we go through kingdom college. For those who are called a different direction, a high school diploma from kingdom high school is fine.

Keep in mind that many extremely mature Christians decide that kingdom college isn't for them and that what they've learned up to this point is where they're to be. It's okay if you know people in this position. If your desire is to journey into the mystical realm of God's ways, expect to be challenged in everything you think you know about the Bible. In kingdom college, we live the Bible, not just read it using head knowledge. In this new season, we move from test to test, allowing each to bring us into greater intimacy with the Trinity. From that intimate place, we understand how life's trials can launch us into a new level of responsibility and maturity.

We explore how kingdom college works using my experience as an example—losing my home through a seven-year eminent domain process. Through my examples, you'll see that the Trinity held my hand and taught me through my freshmen year of kingdom college. That life season lasted the full seven years.

Let's begin with how it all came to pass.

✦

In the summer of 2012, I'm sitting in the middle of a huckleberry patch at the top of a mountain near Priest Lake, Idaho, when my neighbor calls. Normally, I don't pay attention to such calls, but because she's taking care of my cats, I fumble to answer the phone with my berry-stained hands, concerned something is amiss.

"Del! They are building a highway over us! We're going to lose our homes!" she says, bursting into tears.

The day before, a tornado had ripped through Priest Lake, knocking a tree onto my dad's camper. A logger came to the campsite to remove the tree while everyone ogled over his tree-climbing abilities. My dad's camper was totaled, but amazingly, all the electrical, plumbing, and kitchen appliances still worked, so we finished the camping trip. Making light of the situation, one of my brothers called Dad "Captain Crunch" and that we lived in "Crunch Camp."

Already a bit flustered, I talk with my neighbor for a few minutes to get the gist of the story. A Draft Environmental Impact Statement (DEIS) is out, and the contents of those one thousand pages detailed how the state's preferred route will take out our entire community.

In 2012, I didn't know about functioning from the heavenly realms or what I call the come-up-here principle as general protocol. I was part of a dream interpretation school where we practiced prophesying over one another, listening to the heart of the Father for those we prayed with. Somewhere among the words spoken over me, I remembered one prophecy, given in 2010, that talked about how my journey would be like a highway where huge boulders had to be moved and culverts and bridges put in. This would create a nice straight highway.

Upon arriving home from the family camping trip after that fateful phone call, I secure a copy of the DEIS. The specific page is page 181 with a drawing of a bridge crossing over the road near my house. The moment I see the picture, I recall the prophecy. I immediately look it up in my journal and find that it perfectly describes the DEIS picture. What are the odds of that? I know in my spirit that the state of Idaho's preferred route is where this highway will go. I choose not to fight the state as I sense a plan unfolding that is not yet understood.

This journey wasn't easy. In fact, I can honestly say it was one of the most trying events of my life, even more so than my failed marriage. In that situation, I had a choice to stay or leave. In this case, I was at the mercy of the Idaho Transportation Department (ITD). Although I had no idea how this would play out, I made the decision to seek God's plan *in* it. By natural standards, I had every right to be concerned. By God's standards, I had every right to watch him work, partnering with him for the solution. It took me a while to see it, but eventually, I got there.

As you read my story, I share with you the intimate details of my encounters with the Trinity and those in the cloud of witnesses that came alongside me while I learned to function from a heavenly position first. This journey required paradigm shifts, learning an entire new way of thinking, and most of all—trusting God amid what appeared impossible to understand. My hope is that in your own circumstances, you'll find the strength to partner with God and ask him, "What do you have for me *in* this?" When we seek relationship with God as our standard operating procedure, answers come in the strangest ways. Be prepared for anything and everything. Throw religious thinking out the window and get ready to dive into the supernatural world of handling life's circumstances as a student in kingdom college and kingdom graduate school.

CHAPTER 5

Advanced Degrees

BEFORE MOVING ONTO examples, let me introduce you to the advanced degree program in kingdom school. Graduate school starts with a master's degree. A terminal degree is generally the doctorate. Graduate school is much different than undergraduate because the level of responsibility is quite high where students are considered teachers and mentors of those in bachelor's degree programs. This is an introduction to where we can go as we mature further in the things of the kingdom.

A kingdom master's degree is the apprenticeship. A kingdom doctoral degree is taking over the family business and running it. "God and Sons" is Yahweh's business. We are expected to co-labor with him, make decisions, and create together. We are so used to top-down leadership where we aren't required to add our piece because those who are more mature provide what we need.

An example of top-down thinking is when we go to others for prayer or prophetic word. At a conference where I spoke, a young woman came to me, asking for prayer. I said I'd join in agreement with her, but the words needed to come from her. That surprised her, but she agreed to try. We went before Jesus and brought the situation to him. I led her in an exercise where she could see, sense, hear, and feel her interaction with him. All I did was prompt her in the use of her imagination. This was the first time she fully understood how to deal with prayer needs on her own. She was used to seeking out speakers for prayer because like many Christians, she felt leaders have a stronger anointing than she does. This is kingdom grade school thinking. However, it often seeps into the upper levels as well, only because it takes many paradigm shifts to move past this training.

As we advance into the graduate levels, more is expected of us because we've entered the apprenticeship. An apprentice is one who studies a trade under an expert. Recently, the plumber at my house was training a journeyman plumber. A journeyman certificate requires a certain number of hours in order to do a job on your own. The teacher checks the work of an apprentice and approves it. Once the apprentice reaches enough hours, many apprenticeships require an exam. For the kingdom master's program, the Trinity is our journeyman. Once we reach a doctoral program, we are equal partners where we co-create and collaborate (co-labor) with the Trinity in all that we do.

In the kingdom master's program, we apprentice with the Trinity as they show us the ropes. We often see and do things without understanding. Jesus said many times, "I only do what I see my Father do." Here, we watch the Master at work, learning details of how the universe functions. We see a sneak peek of this in kingdom high school and kingdom college. God loves us so much that he can't wait to include us in his job set. Even in the younger grades, just like children, we can do small jobs when we're willing.

Masters and doctoral programs specialize in courses directly related to the major. In both my masters and doctoral programs, I took only music courses. As a performance major, I studied and played music written for clarinet: solos, etudes, chamber music, and orchestral literature. In my master's program, I played the clarinet for ten or more hours per day. My thesis was a recital graded by artist faculty. Since my master's degree was from Yale, many of the teachers taught at Julliard or played in the New York Philharmonic or other major orchestras. They were tough to please. Failing to pass a recital meant the degree wasn't granted.

In a kingdom master's program, our apprenticeship involves learning and understanding everything about the family business, "God and Sons." Here, we do the job with instructions under the Trinity's watchful eye. Kingdom apprenticeship programs have many subjects of study. The major field of study is often based on our life talents, jobs, hardships, hobbies, etc. So what you've gone through in life is useful.

A doctoral program involves deeper specialization. Many music performance doctoral programs expect three recitals, one of which must be a lecture recital. In the sciences, doctoral students work on specific projects under their lead professor. I wrote a dissertation in addition to performing three recitals because my doctoral degree was from the University of Washington, a research institution.

The dissertation is supposed to be about a subject no one else has written about. It's new research with fresh ideas. My dissertation involved looking at the oral cavities of clarinetists through a fiber-optic scope inserted in the corner of the mouth while playing. I theorized that what we think occurs inside the mouth is not actually what's happening. I received major pushback from professional clarinetists and teachers because my hypothesis challenged current performance practices. My study wasn't well accepted and still isn't. At this point, what others say doesn't matter. Their comments don't define me. My students are proof that my techniques work. Why is it that other clarinetists won't listen? They're probably stuck in old paradigms and refuse to see that there may be better and more efficient methods of playing the instrument. We often feel that by giving up old ways of thinking, others believe we're less capable. People who are stuck in religious paradigms have the same issue. Bluntly put, this is an ego problem that should work its way out in kingdom high school. We can't go on to kingdom college and succeed if we're still dealing with our egos.

When we start a kingdom doctoral program, we have ideas that are so new and out-of-the box, many in the Christian community think we're in a cult or, worse yet, going down a rabbit hole that leads directly to the enemy. One of my friends says, "I may not believe tomorrow what I believed yesterday." When we can admit our errors, learn from them, and move on, we're on our way to greater kingdom discoveries. The Trinity can trust us with key principles that dictate how everything in creation functions. We become specialists, training in specific areas so when we come into unity, God's plans are put into action.

My expertise area is frequencies. I look at them from a musical perspective while others do so from a scientific angle. We come together, compare notes, and learn from each other. No one person has the golden ticket because we each provide our special ingredient for the kingdom living recipe.

Do note that our specialist training probably begins in kingdom high school where we decide what we want to be when we grow up. High school was my introduction to studying music as a career. A solid grasp of music theory and the ability to read music is required to understand the deeper concepts of how musical frequencies tie into the whole frequency craze that's sweeping through the kingdom-minded community. Without my musical knowledge, my specialist path may have gone another direction. In kingdom school, the frequency specialty morphed out of my natural training as a musician. Everything you've ever gone through in life will help determine your specialty, which is partly why we learn from our trials and life circumstances.

Not to muddy the waters here, but I must mention that some people function in these higher levels without realizing it. At some point, the puzzle pieces converge into a picture, and the aha moment arrives. At that point, some choose not to continue because it freaks them out or they fear being deceived. If we're solid in godly foundations, our identity in Christ, our authority as a believer, and our call to rule and reign in Christ, the fear of deception is less likely to taunt us. Functioning out of the fear of deception is at the grade school level because we haven't moved past the need for someone more mature than us to provide our spiritual food.

For those who choose a kingdom college path, the door opens for more! We now go through that door as we learn some things about eminent domain.

CHAPTER 6

The Big Meeting

I N SPRING 2013, the ITD held a public hearing at a local hotel so the community could gather to provide input on the rerouting of a small section of Highway 95 south of Moscow, Idaho. State entities set up stations where they handed out brochures and fact sheets and spoke to those who asked questions. Our group meandered around, gathering information. Once the powers that be realized we were the displaced people, they became acutely aware of our presence.

The ITD scheduled two sessions for public input in the largest room. Comments from both sessions appeared in the Final Environmental Impact Statement (FEIS). Our group sat at the back during the first round and listened to members of an environmental group spew off a variety of concerning issues. An earthworm and native grasses seemed more important to them than humans. Being wet behind the ears in all this, I was quite amused by the explosive passionate speeches of many group members. In this first session, our goal was to listen and take in what others said. Proudly wearing T-shirts that read, "You mess with me, you mess with the whole trailer park," we took up two rows of seats, assessing what was unfolding before us. Many gave us curious and inquisitive looks.

Between sessions, we spoke with a variety of experts on all aspects of building highways: noise pollution, the acquisition process, environmental concerns, historic buildings that might be in the right-of-way, the right-of-way process, etc. I knew I had to speak during the second session. After reading the entire DEIS, I understood why the state chose the route that would eventually take my home. In my gut, I knew ITD's chosen route was the best alternative, but here, it appeared to be an environmentalist's heyday. Their voices rang out loud and clear in that first comment session.

About half-way through the second session, I stood up to present my viewpoint. This session was also overrun by the group of environmentalists. But during this session, a TV crew filmed the most flamboyant speakers. People commented until the timer went off while the audience remained quiet. That all changed when I got up. Here I was, one of those being displaced, saying publicly that although I'd lose my home, I agreed with the state's route choice. At the end of my little talk, the audience applauded. From that point on, the atmosphere in the room changed. Those after me began to talk about why they supported the project. Yes, some of that was in the first session too. But for some reason, those comments weren't heard. Not surprisingly, I made it onto the evening news for my thirty seconds of fame.

I discovered later that many who aligned with the environmental group never read the DEIS or FEIS. I asked some of those who disagreed with ITD's decision if they'd read the DEIS. Most hadn't. Their information came from attending meetings where a couple professors from the University of Idaho presented their take on the FEIS. I watched all the videos from those meetings that were posted on someone's YouTube channel. The group's proposed method of fighting ITD came into play as God showed me how to deal with their position in the heavenly courts. This is a perfect example of letting perceived wiser people think for the masses, a phenomenon that occurs outside religious circles as well.

Armed with information, I began the research process into eminent domain laws and how just compensation plays an integral part of relocations. I knew my research was important as I learned to understand the situation through the come-up-here principle. I sensed peace, knowing God had a plan for me during this circumstance. The public hearing in 2013 launched me from kingdom high school into kingdom college.

After the state considered comments from the hearing, ITD issued a FEIS in the fall of 2015. The Federal Highway Administration (FHWA) then issued a Record of Decision (ROD) in March 2016. That prompted a lawsuit by the environmental group, which held up the project for another year. In the fall of 2017, a judge ruled on behalf of the state. The environmental group appealed the ruling. In December 2018, the Ninth Circuit Court held up the decision of the district judge. The highway project could move ahead with full force—nearly seven years after the initial announcement of the DEIS.[4]

When I focused on the situation from my ascended position, I often didn't know if I'd discuss my displacement or other personal issues with the Trinity. The domino effect of developing intimacy spilled into every area of my life, essentially giving me practice in how to view life circumstances through the eyes of God. I was learning about building relationship with the Trinity instead of whining about losing my home.

I continued to stand up for what I felt was right, often because of what I encountered in my times with the Trinity. We don't simply "lie down and take a beating" as some teach. What we do is get the mandate from heaven, administrate it there, then release it to occur on the earth. Sometimes that calls for additional action on our part in the natural, and other times, it's a matter of waiting for more revelation as to what to do and how to do it. I had to be okay with those in the environmental group not liking my position. Although I agreed with the state's route choice, I didn't always agree with how they chose to deal with us as the displaced individuals. The government's idea of just compensation and mine differed.

When there's trouble in River City, we must learn how to handle a problem using the come-up-here principle. Jesus chased out the money changers in the temple. At times, we're called to act in a similar way. I used a barometer of wanting to honor the position without agreeing with the decision.

I didn't mince words with ITD officials when I appealed the original award amount. I went through two real estate agents who didn't believe I'd ever find anything in the price range allotted to me. Time was running short, and the

---

4   "US-95: Thorn Creek Road to Moscow," Idaho Transportation Department, accessed November 21, 2021, https://itdprojects.org/projects/us95thorncreektomoscow.

vacate deadline was quickly approaching. During this time, I realized how well my emotions worked. Although they tried to get the best of me, most of the time, I managed to reign them in while quickly climbing back onto that seat of rest, asking God, "What's going on here?" Then, I'd immediately say, "I trust you. I rest in you. I put on peace. I put on love." Intermixed in all of those emotions, I spent a lot of time praying in tongues.

Waiting seven years to find out where I would be living presented the perfect opportunity for me to walk in faith or fear, especially after losing my highest paying job during it all. Because I didn't know the answer, I struggled with looking for a job. Even during this, God showed me how to trust him. Some of that involved learning how to view provision with a new lens. When we rely solely on our employment as our full source, where's our trust in God? Yes, job security is nice, but sometimes, we might have other ways to financial freedom outside our normal thinking box.

For seven years, every paradigm I held was challenged. How I handled each challenge determined the outcome. Let me repeat that because it is one of the most important keys of this book. How I handled each challenge determined the outcome.

My choices changed the course of how this situation played out. If we keep going around the same mountain, time after time, so that the same junk keeps happening to us, maybe that's a clue that we might need a paradigm shift. I've done that enough to know that if I can see where God is during any circumstance and internalize what I need to learn while I'm there, chances are, I won't go around that mountain again.

Maturing in the middle of life's trials is all about looking directly at each trial and seeing how it can be used to bring us into greater relationship with God and help us mature into well-functioning sons of God. It's a process, just like a kindergartner takes twelve years to eventually learn enough to graduate from high school. Kingdom protocol is no different. Trials and tests take us to new levels of maturity if we allow them to.

I now present a juicy, emotionally charged life trial.

CHAPTER 7

This Is Your House!

"**S**AY THE HOUSE on Lyon Road is yours," Jesus says to me as I drive to work.

"What? How am I going to do that? What if it sells?" I ask.

Silence.

For a moment, I was a little shell-shocked and knew he hadn't answered so that I had a moment to think this through.

I continue, "I need to live by faith. If you say it's mine, then I need to agree with that."

"Hover over it and begin speaking into the land," he instructs.

I wonder, *What am I doing? Is this really God? Am I simply letting my imagination run wild?* I let my thoughts run rampant before I rein them in. Knowing what to do, I ask forgiveness for contrary thoughts, own them, then put them at the feet of Jesus. I then crucify and cover them with the blood of Jesus. As instructed previously, I want to remove unsanctified thoughts from my mind before they became intents.

As I drive, I see my spirit floating above the property. With my free right hand, I wave at it while singing in tongues. My eyes still on the road, my motions mirror what I see with my spiritual eyes. Not knowing what to do,

I sing in tongues to the music playing in my truck for about an hour as I go in and out of seeing this property with my spiritual eyes.

Hearing my thoughts, Jesus says, "Declare and speak over a way to be made for finances."

I begin praying while still hovering over the property. "Father, if you say you're going to make a way, you do. I stand and agree with all that you have for me, including my next house. May all the needed finances be there and may ITD have no issues with my requests. Keep my house safe and away from other buyers. Bless the family who is selling the house with an abundance of finances to meet their needs, above and beyond what they could ask or think. Amen."

I continue to wave my hand while singing in tongues as my spirit goes back and forth over this property. I start to think, *What if. . .* The battle goes on in my mind, and as it does, I continue to focus on living out of faith and seeing God's plan.

"Thank you, Jesus, that I'm learning to hear and then follow through," I speak out.

"These are lessons you continue to learn. You almost missed it because fear started to set in. Let your spirit tell your soul how to respond. Begin to function out of your spirit. Then, your spirit invites your soul into my plan," Father says.

Father, too, is with me as I see the house in the spirit.

"I think that I'm starting to get it. The first thing I wanted to do was blow it off because every other house sold that I had my heart set on. How do I deal with that again?" I ask.

"Those houses were not the houses for you. See from my perspective and take a step forward one day at a time. Learn to stand and see my work be done. Your soul will learn to come in line as you train it to serve the spirit. This is a good exercise for that," instructs Father.

At this point, I have a strong sense to go see the house and stand on the land. I knew God would speak to me there.

✦

What's the kingdom school grade level?

We'll get to the main question about my grade level at the end of this chapter. This next story takes place in my heart garden. I go into greater detail about the garden of the heart in the workbook that accompanies this writing. I encourage you to buy the workbook, especially since I provide the activations I speak of throughout this book.

The house on Lyon Road sold before the relocation process began. At the time, we all thought we'd be gone in the fall of 2016. I kept going back and looking at the online pictures, dreaming how this place could easily fulfill what I'd seen on the scroll (life blueprint) for my new home. Did I hear wrong? I don't think I did. But my version of claiming the house as mine and God's version of that obviously had two different interpretations. Here's what he said to me about that.

I see myself in my heart garden under the Camperdown elm tree. As the river of life flows in front of me, I look out over the landscape where I see huge mountain peaks off in the distance. There is so much light here. Birds chirp and tweet all over, and the fragrance . . . wow! Flowers are all over my garden.

Jesus pokes his head under the branches of the tree, smiling in response to my thoughts.

"Remember, what you smell in earth is often a reflection of what's in heaven," he says.

"Well, it didn't take me too long to realize that fire in my wood stove doesn't smell like gardenias!"

We both laugh.

Looking at me with a serious yet inquisitive eye, he says, "Are you ready to understand a bit more as to why I asked you to claim the house on Lyon Road as yours and then lost it?"

"I'm all ears!" I respond.

Taking my hands in his, he gently says, "My dear, some things are meant for later. They are spirit things that are not necessarily present on earth. That home is a representation of what you have in the kingdom. Just because you thought you lost it, doesn't mean that you actually lost it."

"I'm confused . . . "

"Remember how you hovered over it and declared into the land? It was more about the land than the actual house. What was the goal of the angel that showed up later?"

"Well, I found it interesting that territorial angels showed up during this time. And several things about the north-south direction from Lewiston up to the Canadian border were made evident. Could that have anything to do with it?"

"Remember where that home is located—at the base of Moscow Mountain where the Hoodoo Mountain Range begins. What was on the land couldn't be addressed with people in the house. This then leads to other bits and pieces that connect directly to Highway 95, which then leads through the entire state of Idaho. Do you see the connection now?" Jesus says, leaning in toward me.

"If I understand correctly, this is not about a physical home on physical land. It's more about opening a spiritual connection along a route that needs opening that then frees something that has to do with this highway. Is that close?" I ask.

For a moment, Jesus smiles, soaking in my words. We look deeply into each other's eyes.

"You think this situation is about you and your relocation, or at least, that's what you thought in the beginning. As you've learned, this is strategic. At the same time, it brought you to a new level of maturity. Since you are losing a home, you are now given authority in spiritual matters concerning the highway project. The home on Lyon Road represents a spiritual position. It stayed on the market long enough for you to accomplish what was needed in the spirit. So, you didn't lose the home. You had spiritual access to it for the time you needed that access. That couldn't be done with people living in it."

I ponder this for another moment. *So, in a sense, what happened in the spirit on this property set the stage for the next series of events to play out?*

"Exactly!" Jesus exclaims, answering my thoughts. "Remember, what people think is something in the natural is actually to be done in the spirit. That part, you did. But you misinterpreted the part about believing this house would physically be yours."

✦

Now to determine our grade levels for the story. What we often think is meant for one thing has another purpose. When we look at situations with our natural eyes, we don't see how God will use that situation to accomplish the plan. In this area of my life, I functioned at the maturity of upper grade school. I'm learning that when we look outside ourselves amid our circumstances, we see a more expansive picture. God uses life events to invite us into a new level of maturity.

I asked the big "why?" question in this incident but was met with silence at first. In my own standard thinking, I believed that I'd missed it, which is grade school thinking. I understood that there was a purpose in the situation but didn't comprehend that purpose until later.

In kingdom school, the door of faith opens, which in turn allows the supernatural aspect to be loosed. If we're going to function at a high school kingdom level, we move past viewing life from a natural and worldly perspective. In this story, I functioned in kingdom grade school because of the "it's all about me" mentality. When we focus our own issues instead of on the bigger picture, we are still in grade school.

The house on Lyon Road is at the base of the Hoodoo Mountain range. I needed to take care of something specific about that spot in the spirit. At the time, it didn't make sense. I can see Hoodoo Mountain out my front window from my current house. I'm now at the northern end of the range. What are the odds of that? I was strategically placed in both positions for reasons that are being revealed to me as I continue my journey.

I encourage you to read Chapter 2, "Dealing with Familiar Spirits" in *Maturing as a Mystic: Workbook.* Because I go through a process thinking that I messed up in the above story, this might be a good time to read about familiar spirits.

CHAPTER 8

The Come-Up-Here Principle

COMPREHENSION OF THIS principle begins in kingdom college. We have tastes of it throughout all grade levels, but here, we learn to function in it as our go-to method of operating. We sit with the Trinity, create a plan together, then administrate it on earth. At times, the plan is all about bringing us to another level of maturity. Because God knows it takes us a while to think like him, the plan is often a test. If we pass, great! If we don't, there's a do-over. I've rarely heard God say to me, "Are you ready for a tough test?" When he does ask that question, I know it's for a specific purpose, which he usually outlines in a discussion. In cases like the house on Lyon Road, I went through a natural progression of grasping concepts.

We often don't know the purpose of a circumstance or what our role is through it. Unless we learn to see situations from a heavenly perspective first, we can easily miss the opportunity that goes along with the circumstance. That circumstance might be the one thing that can change an entire community even if it feels like the focus is on us. If we have a woe-is-me attitude, we can misinterpret *how* God can use us during a situation.

When I first learned about the highway project, I functioned from an earthly perspective more so than heavenly. Because our bodies are the temple of the Holy Spirit, God is as close as the air we breathe (1 Corinthians 6:19), so why do we need to continue inviting his presence to come flood our spaces? He's already done that. With the come-up-here principle, we function in him so we can see situations from a higher perspective. We can't do that when we're in ourselves.

One of my favorite pictures of a higher perspective is demonstrated through lookout towers. If you're not familiar with the West Coast of the United States, before satellite imagery and modern technology, the US Forest Service positioned lookout towers on top of mountains so they could spot fires. Forest Service personnel manned those lookouts twenty-four hours a day, seven days a week, all summer long. Since my father worked for the forest service, we spent a lot of time in the Idaho woods every summer.

We can quickly spot danger from a high position. Then, we can easily put out any fires that send up smoke signals, thinking they're being a bit sneaky. So the come-up-here principle adds another layer of sight to our Christian walk. Rick Joyner talks about going up a mountain in his book *The Final Quest*.[5] In his book, the higher he goes, the farther away he gets from the enemy and the better he sees from God's perspective. When we resonate with the presence of God, that overrides what the Accuser tries to bring.

The first time that I understood losing my home was more than just about me, I was a bit surprised. My focus was on me, which is grade school thinking. I then remembered the prophecy that described my life as a highway. However, I thought the prophecy was preparing me for the move. Enter from stage right—paradigm shifts in thinking outside the box.

I began to understand on a much deeper level how to ascend, as many people now call it. We choose words that work for people, and ascending provides a strong pictorial image. It took more than a year to recognize the connections between the highway project and how God desired to use the situation for specific purposes. By now, I was well into kingdom high school because it was no longer all about me. God used my moving experience to bring me into a greater understanding of how to function in the come-up-here principle.

In a journal entry from March 2016, I noted, "In seeking God, I realize one of the reasons the ROD came out when it did was because God wanted to

5   Rick Joyner, *The Final Quest* (Fort Mill, SC: Morningstar Publications, 2006).

give me an opportunity to learn and function in his government so it can be administrated in this situation." During this encounter with God, gold dust from my cloak (in the spirit) fell on the land. I was instructed to release the blessings of God over the land and then go on my way. It was short, sweet, and simple.

In May 2016, the Holy Spirit instructed me to put together a packet of research for ITD that directly related to my living situation, what I wanted in a new home, and what I expected from ITD in the process. In August 2016, the relocation team met with the homeowners and gave us a rundown of the process. Things in the spirit didn't begin to shift until that meeting. Here, I functioned at the kingdom high school level. By kingdom high school, most Christians are adept at hearing and sensing the voice of God. We transition from natural mindsets to spiritual thinking.

We move now to an example where I was invited to the throne room of God in the early stages of my journey while I waited for my relocation package from ITD.

✦

From the throne, a voice speaks. "You are going to learn more about what's on your destiny scroll. More will be unlocked before you so you're ready to receive when it happens. Once you have an understanding, it's important to begin taking natural steps toward what you see through revelation. This includes seeing it fulfilled, dreaming about it, envisioning it happening and then holding it in your heart just as you're doing with your new home. I will show you more plans about that house too. Be prepared and ready to stand on my Word."

A rumbling comes from the throne. A scroll appears and levitates in front of the throne. "Take it!" says the voice, which I know is Father (Yahweh). The light coming from Father is overwhelmingly bright, so I stare at the scroll. A very large and majestic angel takes the scroll and brings it to me.

"In this scroll are instructions and blueprints of what's in store for you in this next season," says Father. "Out of it comes much of what you're called to do. That revelation stems from building relationship with me. My people need to learn how to practice with patience and perseverance just like you've had posted in your studio for years. They also need to learn not to be 'weenies,' as you also state."

The room erupts in laughter and joy at these words. I do have a way with words.

Father continues, "Everything you've learned as a classical musician is reflected in how my kingdom works. It is true in other disciplines too. As my people realize this, they will have a better understanding of the cost associated with what it takes to walk with me. That cost many speak about is simply giving up what takes attention off us as the Trinity, the things that feed the flesh. To function out of your spirit, you must listen to my words, be *in me*, and let the River of Glory flow out of you. People can't do that if their eyes are on the things of the world. As you've already discovered, people numb themselves by spending hours doing what entertains them. What is in my kingdom brings life."

I ponder on this for a moment, thinking of the many things I've done to numb my mind, like watching TV.

"TV is part of my creation," says Father. "I use it to get my word to people. However, it's like a gun; it can be used for evil as well as for good. If you become fixated with TV, then it becomes an idol."

I know this is true as I think back to when I'd sit in front of it for hours just because I didn't want to think about life issues. What I was watched was okay. However, it took time away from Father when he was trying to speak to me. And I would say, "I know God's speaking but don't know how to listen." Hmmm…

Again, hearing my thoughts, Father says, "It's not the thing (TV) that's the issue; it's when it becomes an idol, and you spend time with it rather than in our presence. It's no different than people who leave the TV or radio on all day for white noise. Words are important because they carry a frequency and creative force."

Changing direction, Father continues, "Favor will be on you exactly when it needs to be. Stay in our presence so when the time is right, you're ready to step into what's needed for that moment. You will already be prepared and can then easily step right where you're supposed to be with ease. Although, some things, I may not show you until after you're in place. It's not always about having all your little ducks in a row. You must learn to walk in faith while you prepare."

By now, I'm on my face before Father. The Seven Spirits of God are on both sides of me. I still can't see their features, but I know they are with me to tutor me and show me what I need to know as I begin this next season of instruction.

"Get up!" I hear Father say. "Stand in my glory and let it flow through you so that it gives you strength and courage to carry out your scroll of testimony on earth."

I stand and see the scroll hover before me. Taking it in my hands, I open it up and see writing in a language that I don't understand.

From the throne, I hear, "You will begin to understand as you walk with us. Now, eat it!"

I take the scroll, roll it back up and begin to eat. As I do, imagery flows through my mind, things I've been shown over the last few months. I have no frame of reference for this sweet taste. The more I eat, the more I want it!

Father continues, "Worship and begin to strategize as you get revelation. Write it all down. Revisit some of the previous experiences for more clarification."

"Thank you for your love and revelation. I accept all you've shown me and ask the Holy Spirit and Seven Spirits of God, along with my angels, to help me carry out what's on this scroll," I bow low before Father.

✦

What's the kingdom school grade level?

In the above encounter, I stepped out by faith without understanding it fully. I wasn't dealing with doubt, fear, or anything that kept me from receiving the revelation put before me. In this case, I functioned out of the beginning stages of kingdom college where I had an encounter but didn't understand it yet. In the supporting workbook, I present further details about scrolls.

Until I'm released to share my encounters with the public, I don't. That's a new level of maturity for me because as a young adult, I struggled with keeping my mouth shut. Boasting is functioning from kingdom middle school because middle schoolers are learning to step into their identity and they like to show off. I was the queen show-off in middle school. People are excited and want to share all they're learning. However, not everyone is ready to hear at that moment. We need to be wise in how and when we share our encounters.

Everything we do in kingdom college comes from cultivating relationship with God (Yahweh), Jesus (Yeshua), and the Holy Spirit. As this becomes our plumb line, everything else falls into place. I liken this process to purchasing a home that needs major remodeling, tearing it down to bare studs, then rebuilding it using fresh materials. The foundation is solid, but what's built on that foundation needs work. Jesus talks about this in Matthew 7:24–27 where the foolish man builds his house on the sand and a wise man builds it on rock. We gain firm foundations through studying truths in the Bible as our guide to live life in Christ, build character, and function in the fruit of the Spirit where love is of utmost importance (I Corinthians 13–14).

I encourage you to read chapter 1, "The Imagination" from *Maturing as a Mystic: Workbook*. I go into greater detail about how to use a sanctified imagination in an ascension experience. In addition, I provide a "seeing" exercise for you to practice daily.

CHAPTER 9

Wasteland of the Unknown

U PON RECEIPT OF the relocation papers, we were given six months to find a home and move. At the time, few houses were on the market in Moscow, Idaho, where I lived. The ones that were available were out of my price range unless ITD changed their procedure for the allocation of funds. When a relocation specialist hand-delivered my offer, it was much lower than I expected. I was not a happy camper! Her response was, "Well, you got more than we've ever awarded anyone else in your situation." Yeah, like that made me feel any better. I was functioning out of middle school here because my emotions were all over the place. I eventually reined them in, but that took some time.

ITD knew I'd lost my highest paying job because I couldn't commit to a ten-month contract. When I asked ITD prior to signing the contract when I'd have to move, they indicated it would be before the end of the school year. That's what I told my boss, so she decided to hire someone else. That left my sole source of income as a part-time teaching job in Spokane, Washington. ITD essentially based my relocation package on finding a home in Washington, not Idaho.

By now, I was backed into a corner where I had no choice but to see the entire relocation through the eyes of the Trinity. They had me right where I needed to be. It was extremely uncomfortable and unsettling. I was operating at a grade level that encompassed K–12 thinking because I was still looking at the situation with my natural eyes. I flip-flopped back and forth across many grade levels as I learned new protocols. Remember what I said about freshmen in college and how they acted? Yeah, this is the kind of stuff they do.

By now, I realized I'd be leaving Moscow and heading further north. Where that was, I had no clue. I couldn't find a real estate agent to work with me because none of them understood the relocation paperwork. They all said no houses were on the market in my price range. Growing pains are not easy, but now that I'm nearly three years past the big move, I can see how it launched me into a new season.

By the middle of January 2019, I had less than three months left to find a home *and* move. I placed an offer on a fixer-upper in Post Falls, Idaho, but because the bank owned it, they were in no hurry to decide which offer to accept. On January 5, while discussing the matter with the Trinity, Jesus said, "Go look on Craigslist." The moment I opened the "homes for sale" category, a home in Oldtown, Idaho, appeared in the first few listings—in my price range. It had been posted just ten hours earlier. With the relocation specialist in tow, I met the owner on January 11. The moment I walked into the house, I knew it was mine. The move-in date was scheduled for February 12, 2019. Although I was moving to a town that I knew nothing about, that wasn't my concern at this point. I finally had a home.

With that introduction, we back up a bit to the fall of 2018 around the time I received my relocation papers. As you read the stories, can you determine which grade level(s) I'm functioning from?

✦

"Father, I know everything about this highway project can be used to help me grow and mature. I receive all that I'm to learn in this situation. I step into your presence before the court. I repent for carrying this burden by taking it back when something new and stupid happens. Help me understand how to operate out of rest."

"You're forgiven," says Papa.

A large gavel comes down, reverberating as it hits something.

"Don't allow people's behavior to determine your responses," says Elijah, who comes up to stand beside me. "It's all about choices."

"Thank you for that reminder," I say, turning to greet him.

Together, we leave the courtroom. Almost instantly, we're under the Camperdown elm tree next to the River of Life in the garden of my heart. We sit quietly as we watch the rainbow fish "swim" down the river. Now that I know they are scrolls, it finally makes sense. They jump into me.

Elijah laughs at that thought. We both giggle as we continue to sit quietly.

"Our response determines the outcome," Elijah says after a moment of silence. "That being said, at least you didn't rip ITD a new one in your last email."

"I did ponder for a while about what to say. I don't want to attack people, but at what point do I call things as they are to their faces?" I ask.

"There is a key," Jesus says as he joins the conversation. "It's all about you heart attitude. Let's look at your attitude while you wrote the email. Were you frustrated?"

"Yes," I responded.

"Did you attack ITD?" Jesus questioned.

"No. I wanted to be as respectful as possible."

"Were you wrong?"

"I got out of peace. However, I did have a moment where I wanted to pummel someone."

Elijah and Jesus both laugh at that comment.

"Was there maturity?" Elijah asks.

"Yes," I respond. "I wasn't as pissed off as usual."

"Maturity comes through being presented circumstance to practice. No, you weren't disrespectful in your responses. You did struggle with responding in peace," Jesus offers.

"That's obviously hard for me," I answer. "My problem is that stupid stuff keeps coming at me. I've gone to court, released matters, held people in my heart, and released all kinds of angelic help over the situation. However, nothing appears to be making a difference. That's what's frustrating."

"What are you learning?" Jesus asks.

"To trust more in you," I answer.

"And that brings you into greater relationship."

"Yes. That alone makes it worth it," I add.

"Bless those who come against you. Then, watch God work on your behalf," Elijah instructs me.

"Said from the mouth of a true wise man," Jesus interjects.

Without further prompting, I stand in the spirit and begin to declare. "I release blessings over ITD and those that are responsible for my relocation. I say that peace and joy surround them. May they have rich time with no extra stress to prepare documents that have been created in heaven first. May they hear the heart of God for me and my neighbors. I speak peace and joy over their lives and that they would all come to greater knowledge of who God is."

Several angels come to capture my words. Looking like many balls of light, they speed off to deliver what I've declared.

✦

What's the kingdom school grade level?

Three grade levels are at play here. Everything involving squirrely emotions is at the middle school level. When I write the appeal letter to ITD, I'm functioning out of a high school level because I understand my authority as a believer. Kingdom high school is all about understanding what's in the Bible and administrating from that position. I'd done my research and reminded ITD of what was in their own documents. I knew in my spirit that I needed to keep them aware of their own rules. That was kingdom college thinking because I discussed these issues with the Trinity prior to writing the letter. However, my *attitude* needed an adjustment during the process. I flip-flopped between middle school, high school, and college based on attitudes and actions.

I also functioned at the grade school level in this encounter because I was very focused on what I was going to do. Look for the "me" and "I" statements, actions, and reactions. Remember that grade school kids are very self-focused and struggle with seeing beyond that. Grade school includes a woe-is-me attitude. In more churchy words, this is a victim mentality.

Elijah is part of the cloud of witnesses that I see quite often. The cloud of witnesses are sent to tutor and train us in the ways of God so that we can learn from their same mistakes. I mention more about scrolls in this story and include an activation on scrolls in the supporting workbook.

I encourage you to read Chapter 4, "Being Yoked with Christ" in *Maturing as a Mystic: Workbook*. As we step from kingdom grade school into high school, being yoked with the Trinity makes the transition a bit easier. I provide a daily activation to assist with understanding this "in him" principle.

CHAPTER 10

The Art of Frustration

A S I SIT on the bench next to the river of life sitting with the Trinity, I ponder my relocation.

"Is this what it's like when there's no place to turn to?" I ask. "I literally have no direction. Although I put feelers out there, including looking for jobs, nothing seems right. I need help!"

I stare straight ahead, my mind blank. What am I missing?

Jesus pulled me closer to him. Then Papa and Holy Spirit drew closer as well. I feel as if I am in the middle of a sandwich.

"Are you ready to listen?" asks Jesus.

"I thought I was listening," I offer.

"Sometimes, expectations get in the way because they cloud thinking. They also skew what you do in the spirit. Not that what you did was wrong. However, there was an expected outcome," Jesus says.

Papa adds, "When you have expected outcomes, you miss the smallest of directives that could lead another way."

"You know my heart," I reply, looking toward each of them. "I want what's best by seeing through your eyes."

We sit in silence as Jesus smiles at me.

"Please forgive me for doing this out of my own strength," I continue. "I repent for harboring pre-conceived ideas about what I thought the outcome should be. How do I proceed?"

"Stay in a place of rest in this," Jesus answers.

"I don't understand how to do that, especially when nothing appears to make sense," I offer.

"Look at me!" Jesus says, grabbing my head and turning it toward him. "Now, what are you doing?"

"Looking at you," I answer.

"Exactly! That's how you respond when you don't understand. In me, together, we come up with solutions," Jesus says cheerfully yet sternly at the same time.

"Growth by trial," I quip.

"There really isn't a better way. If everything comes so easily, it will keep you from maturing," Papa interjects.

I continue to look into Jesus's eyes. I know that I don't have the answers, but this is where my focus has to remain.

✦

What's the kingdom school grade level?

This was 100 percent functioning out of both grade school and middle school. Everything about this encounter screamed, "I'm so emotional that I can't get my head on straight." Notice that I was self-focused and concerned that God didn't appear to be understanding my pleas. In a sense, it was fine that the emotions kicked in because they were stunted during the abusive marriage. In one sense, this was maturity, but I needed to reign my emotions in better. Squirrely emotions aren't necessarily negative. However, when we allow them to continue ruling us, issues can arise. By the end, my focus was on Jesus's eyes. If our gaze stays there, we're in the right place.

When we have expected outcomes, we are operating out of high school because we need greater comprehension skills to build expectations. Therefore, we can possibly function in several grade levels at the same time. As we mature, growing in God's character and integrity, this phenomenon occurs less and less. We play catch-up, just like some college students who must take remedial classes during their freshmen year.

I encourage you to read Chapter 3, "First Chamber of the Heart – the Garden" in *Maturing as a Mystic: Workbook*. I found that as I spent more time in my heart garden, I was more able to keep my head on straight when life situations got tough. I include a daily activation that takes you on a journey of exploring your own heart garden.

CHAPTER 11

Words Carry Weight

AS I SPEND time with the Trinity, our times together involve many lessons in how the kingdom functions. My latest lesson brings us back to the Camperdown elm tree for some time by the River of Life. It's been a while since we hovered over my property, and now it's time to ask more questions.

"I'm not sure what is going on with this move," I speak out. "I'm trying to be in that place of rest, waiting for the right timing. It would be nice to have some strategy."

Jesus looks at me with soft and loving eyes. He says, "There are times for strategy and times for waiting. You're in a waiting time, but even in that, there's strategy. So many pieces must fall together for that one piece that's still needed—in this case, your new home. What may seem like a disaster to you is an alignment of the needed pieces. You do well to stay in that place of rest."

"I'm not always so good at staying in that place," I offer. "My job! I don't even know where to start with that one!"

"You did ask that I close the doors that need to be closed and to open the doors that need to be open. Is that correct?" he asks.

"I did."

"Remember, the prayers of a righteous man avail much. What you say carries weight. Don't wade through too much muck."

We giggle at that as I let it soak in. I don't want to put my efforts into something that's wastable.

Jesus continues, "Things are still in the alignment process. It's important to continue decreeing what you need and desire over your situation. Let's go over your list."

As I write it down, I speak it out: 1) All my cats are welcome in my new home. 2) I own my land. 3) I have a home large enough for a recording studio and guests who want to stay. 4) My outdoor projects are allowed, and the home is not close to a wheat field. It also has a large living room. 5) My home is within an hour of my job in Spokane. 6) A shop and/or garage is a bonus. 7) I will have a job that's flexible with my teaching and traveling schedule.

"Never underestimate the power of a decree!" Jesus says after I read my list. "Now, decree this over ITD as well."

✦

What's the kingdom school grade level?

As in the previous encounter, two grade levels are at play here. I specifically asked God to close doors that needed to be closed. My prayer, said in faith, was at a high school level. Words create life and death where what we speak, we live from. Based on my own life experiences, we spend kingdom high school comprehending the power of our words. We learn to use biblical truths in how we function. If we don't solidify these concepts, we struggle in kingdom college and will need to deal with some remedial coursework. People often spend time in their freshmen year of kingdom college adjusting mindsets concerning biblical truths and godly protocols.

The section where I decree is also at the high school level. Again, I am using the power of words in Scripture to bring about a thing. I step into kingdom college here as well because I'm creating the decrees from my position in Christ, looking through his eyes. In a sense, I'm seeing into the future. Together, we looked at the details. Out of those details came the decrees. What I decreed came to pass within a month! Let's revisit the decrees.

1. *All my cats are welcome in my new home.* This came true because of the next decree. Had I moved to another trailer park, I would have been allowed only two cats.
2. *I own my land.* I purchased a "stick-built" home on my own land, which allowed me to do what I wanted with my property. There are no neighborhood covenants.
3. *I have a home large enough for a recording studio and guests who want to stay.* I now have five bedrooms and three bathrooms in this home! There's also a dedicated space for recording.
4. *My outdoor projects are allowed, and the home is not close to a wheat field. It also has a large living room.* I created one larger shed built from all the doors in two sheds that I had in Moscow. I live in a forested area, and I have a very large living room.
5. *My home is within an hour of my job.* It takes fifty minutes to get to work.
6. *A shop and/or garage is a bonus!* It has a garage that I've transformed into a retreat center where I still have some garage space.
7. *I will have a job that's flexible with my teaching and traveling schedule.* I haven't had to get a second job. I'm learning more about provision from a heavenly perspective. Eventually, I'll share more about this in another book.

I encourage you to read "Chapter 13: Life Scrolls" in *Maturing as a Mystic: Workbook*. Since this chapter (in this book) is about speaking into the future, it's a great time for you to explore what's on your life scroll. I provide a daily activation to help you discover what's inherently built into your life design. Think about all the things you love to do, your job skills, hidden talents, and more as you prepare to read about scrolls.

CHAPTER 12

A Sneak Peek into the Future

I CONTINUE TO PONDER over my housing situation as I sit near the River of Life. My focus must be on the Trinity, not the circumstance. I've written another appeal after finding nothing on the market in my price range. I don't see in the natural how provision will come for my relocation. I'm stymied as I continue to think while watching the rainbow fish swim around. One jumps into my lap and then goes into my belly. I thank it, knowing it carries another scroll that I will eventually understand. Jesus chuckles as he pokes his head under the tree.

"Enjoying the bench?" he asks.

"I continue to marvel at the things in the kingdom. Nothing ceases to amaze me!" I answer. "Although I don't enjoy life's dirty little circumstances, I'm closer to you through them."

"And that, my friend, is where many people fail," Jesus responds. "They think they can handle life on their own when things go well."

Papa joins us and takes a seat on the other side of me. My focus turns to their eyes. As I continue to look, I step in and become part of the vision. I want to understand my current situation by being in Christ. From this position, it's like we're staring into a Google earth map where I can zoom in and out of various places around the globe. Angels are lined up everywhere, waiting for direction from the sons of God. We zoom into my current neighborhood sometime in the future.

"Shall we follow the moving truck?" Jesus asks.

"First, you need to decree and declare some things," Papa instructs. "You've done all the research and have an idea of where you'd like to be. From this point in time, decree what you desire. Then, carry that into the future. As we're in this together, you'll know which choices are more profitable for you than others. Look. See. Then decree."

Maybe I've looked at this from a poverty mentality, thinking ITD's latest rejection is the final answer. For that mindset, I repent and step into faith, receiving all the provision God has for me in this move.

"I like a couple of communities in the Post Falls area: Hauser, Oldtown, and possibly Spirit Lake. I want to own my land," I offer.

"Decree it!" instructs Papa.

"I decree that I will move to my own piece of land somewhere along Highway 53 or Highway 41 with my name as the title holder." As I decree, all of us hover above the area I'm speaking over.

"Now, release that decree into the atmosphere over this land," Jesus instructs.

I continue, "I take this decree from the kingdom realms and release it over the land. I also say the heart of the current homeowner is prepared to work with me through the uniqueness of this situation. I ask the angelic to deliver the decree to the owner."

"Well done!" exclaims Papa. "Shall we go back to your current land in the future?"

No sooner are the words out of his mouth then we are hovering above my current home, watching the movers load the truck. They take off, heading north on Highway 95. My camper trailer is still on the property. The door sheds are still assembled, but everything in them is gone.

We follow the large moving truck, hovering way above it. Surrounding the movers is an army of the angelic. In what seems like no time, we pull up to the city of Hauser. I then lose track of where the truck goes.

"Why can't I see that?" I ask.

"There needs to be more paradigm shifts not just in words but in action," Papa answers. "You can't be moved by what you see in the natural. You must operate out of faith. As you do, revelation comes."

"Is it because I was negative after receiving the rejection to my appeal?" I ask.

"Yes," answers Jesus. "It was only for a short time, but that did lead to other thoughts, which created the actions."

Immediately, I know what to do.

"I own and repent for the 'oh crap! What am I going to do?' attitude. I renounce all ties to that and the following actions. I crucify it and cover it with the blood of Jesus. I trade stinking thinking and actions for the truth, revelation, and wisdom as I move forward in this process."

"As you continue to walk this out, you'll see more. Build up faith and stand by the decrees. You'll also know when you step foot on the land which house is for you. That's why you're not seeing it now. It's not ready to be seen."

✦

What's the kingdom school grade level?

This encounter demonstrates two levels of maturity: kingdom grade school and kingdom college. The grade school level is the "what am I going to do?" attitude. I repent so that circumstances can move forward again. When we get into this mindset, we are looking for natural resolutions to natural circumstances. Obviously, my focus wasn't in the right place, and it had a consequence; I couldn't see past a certain point because I needed a paradigm shift. Notice there is teaching and redirection here. It's a training ground for me to move into greater levels of maturity and responsibility.

Kingdom college training occurred when we hovered over the different lands. I know what we did in this encounter was accurate because it played out exactly as we saw it. I moved further north, not far from Highway 41. When hovering above my home in Moscow, the moving trucks loaded as described. They came and packed up the house and door sheds first. The camper didn't leave right away. The door sheds weren't disassembled and moved until later.

I encourage you to read "Chapter 8: Our Personal Mountain" in *Maturing as a Mystic: Workbook*. The mountain of our life is where we "rule and reign" over personal situations and circumstances. From this place, we're seated in Christ and can learn to be at rest and peace despite what goes on around us. I provide a daily activation that leads you in discovering what's on your personal mountain.

CHAPTER 13

Accusations in Court

I STEP INTO THE court with Jesus at my side. Father is behind the bench, and the Accuser is also seated in his place on the witness stand. Several of the cloud of witnesses file in. I see Elijah, David, and Moses—all of whom I've worked with on several occasions. As more beings continue to file in, my personal angel is with me along with Chief Tall Feather, Moscow's angel. Two other regional angels enter as well. These angels have been with me during the entire relocation process as we work on cleaning up the land and preparing for the highway project to move forward. After everyone takes their seats, Father motions for me to come forward.

"State your case," Father requests.

"I'm here to present my just compensation case," I speak.

"Are there any accusations keeping this from moving forward?" he asks.

"I have the list here," answers the Accuser.

"Read them," Father says sternly.

The Accuser begins to read out loud. "Fear of losing her rights. Fear of being overlooked. Lack of faith and trust where she's paying attention to the opposition. Believing lies about what's due to her. Trust in her own resources and ideas. Working on this in her own strength. Not trusting for provision. Debauchery."

I listen to the list as it's read, knowing they are spot on except for the last one. It doesn't matter. Someone in my ancestral line has obviously done it, so I choose to cover the accusation.

"How do you plead?" Father asks me.

"Guilty on all charges," I state. The moment I accept the charges, the Accuser disappears.

"You are forgiven," Father says as the gavel comes down.

"May I also request a divorce decree?" I ask.

"Granted!" replies Father as he hands me a scroll. "Now, let's get down to the real business at hand. What is your request?"

"I petition the court to rule in my favor on my relocation for this highway project. United States law allows for just compensation when a home is taken by eminent domain. Interpretations vary, but I do have a definition that I feel justly compensates my situation."

Father motions for me to bring it forward. I step up to the bench and hand him the paperwork. He looks over it before handing it back to me. However, he suddenly has his own copy.

"Please read it," he instructs.

"Based on various interpretations of US law, those within eminent domain situations are eligible for just compensation. I ask the court to enact the definition in this paperwork for my situation. That definition states 'a full and perfect equivalent for the property taken. That includes land type, allowable privileges, financial obligations, and ability to function as if the taking never occurred.'"

Whispering comes from behind me. Father reviews the paperwork.

"What makes you feel that you deserve this?" Father asks.

"Your Word says that you care for every hair on my head. Proverbs 6:31 also says that what the enemy steals from me, he must replace seven-fold. In this case, if I go by ITD's ruling, I'll lose all my current privileges and have double the monthly payments. I consider that stealing because it takes away my current standard of living. If anything, I believe this is a case for an upgrade to a stick home on my own land, not a rented lot. Yes, I could go live in another trailer park. However, I consider the loss of my ability to work from home or have all my cats or practice whenever I want to a stealing of my current standard of living. I put you in remembrance of your Word that also says when we ask anything, believing by faith, it's given to us. According to some interpretations of US law, some legal systems would agree with my definition of just compensation. Continuing in a similar situation where I lose none of my current privileges makes me 'justly compensated.' Having my own piece of land is crucial because I can't have what I need if I am living in another trailer park because their rules don't allow it."

Father smiles as he looks at the territorial angels. I know this is more about my ability to remember what's in his Word and to learn to stand on those truths.

"Is there anything else to be done on or with this land before I give my ruling?" he asks the angels.

"All is well and complete," answers Chief Tall Feather, the chief angel over Moscow. The others nod in agreement.

"Done!" Father announces as he pounds down the gavel.

He hands me a scroll with the decree and pounds the gavel again to indicate court is dismissed.

✦

What's the kingdom school grade level?

The entire encounter is kingdom college level. This court case was prepared with help from the Trinity, the cloud of witnesses, and territorial angels who were in attendance. I wasn't functioning out of any residual emotional issues that clouded my ability to see. When the charges were read, I accepted all of them without arguing. The Accuser is the Accuser. He sneaks in matters that affect us because a previous generation hasn't dealt with them. I learned early on to accept all accusations. If I haven't done it, someone in my generational line did. I want freedom for everyone in my family, so I repent anytime an accusation comes against me because not only does it free me, my whole family benefits as well.

The result of this case is outlined in my decrees from the previous chapter. The court case was to deal with the spiritual things behind how ITD viewed just compensation. I was given a supernatural view of what was happening behind the scenes. According to Ephesians 6:2, we don't war against issues in the natural (flesh and blood). We deal with evil forces in the heavenly realms as standard operating procedure. In this instance, I did that through a court case.

When we only use Scripture in a process without including the Trinity's input for specific applications, we are operating from the kingdom high school level. Again, for lack of a better term, the ascension process that I label the come-up-here principle is the key in functioning in kingdom college. This goes beyond what we learned in the Bible because it's real time interaction where we apply Scripture from the heavenly perspective.

I had to get a blueprint for this court case. I prepared it in advance based on encounters with the Trinity. They instructed me on how to move forward. I went to Scripture looking for protocol that I could add to strengthen my case. By seeing the entire highway project through Jesus's eyes, I learned things I wouldn't have known otherwise. I probably wouldn't have even researched just compensation had the Trinity not pointed out key concepts of this to me. This is what living in the kingdom realms is all about—real time walking with the Trinity. In kingdom college, we learn to function from this position in our daily lives. The relocation was my introduction to kingdom college. God uses whatever life circumstance we're walking through to bring us full-time into functioning in him. We can't do that unless we're willing to live out of the come-up-here principle.

In the accompanying workbook, I present information in Chapter 12 about epigenetic switches and how they affect our ancestral line. This comes into play when we step into the mobile court. It's why I accepted the accusations here.

As with all kingdom college lessons, they challenge our belief systems. If we're not challenged, then we have minimal forward motion into a greater level of maturity. If I can reiterate one thing; trials are meant to mature us. Whining is not a viable option. Step into the lesson, learn from it, then advance to the next lesson. If we continue to whine, we may repeat the lesson.

I encourage you to read the chapters on the garden of your heart in *Maturing as a Mystic: Workbook*. The purpose of our heart garden is to bring us into greater alignment with the character of God. This means that we come into agreement with his epigenetics, not those of our human ancestors.

Postlude

WE HAVE ALL had life experiences that create trauma and hardships. Those experiences can create thought processes that stunt us. This is one reason we're told to take every thought captive. (See 2 Corinthians 10:5.) Negativity, fear, worry, anxiety, depression, anger, and all their cuddle buddies are born out of thoughts first. When we reign in our thought life, negative thoughts don't rule our actions. The more we entertain stinking thinking, the more it directs our actions. Practiced actions lead to habits and established paradigms.

When we become Christ followers, we can heal from life events and the related issues. If we don't work through them in kingdom middle school or high school, we get to take remedial training in college. Here's a reminder from the book *Kingdom Shift: How to Prepare for God's Global Reset.* [6] I provide a list in how we can function. I've amended the list I shared in the prelude and added grade levels as well.

- Allow God to lead. Consider prophecies and teachings but don't allow them to guide us in place of personal interaction with the Trinity. When we focus on prophetic words and others' teachings as our guide to live life, we are functioning in kingdom grade school. This is the milk of the Word.

---

6   Del Hungerford, *Kingdom Shift: How to Prepare for God's Global Reset* (Idaho: Healing Frequencies Music, 2020), 41.

- Don't look to the right or left. Keep our eyes on God the entire time despite circumstances. We tend to start comprehending this in the later years of kingdom grade school.
- Learn to see everything from a position of love. See people who treat us poorly, including governmental leaders, through God's love filter. This is protocol at every level.
- Don't allow circumstances to rule emotions. Functioning out of emotions is kingdom middle school.
- Stay in a place of rest and peace no matter what happens. This is kingdom high school protocol. However, we start the lessons in rest and peace much earlier.
- Keep short accounts. This protocol is practiced at all levels—some with higher comprehension than others.
- Repent and forgive as needed. Repentance keeps the enemy at bay so that emotions don't fester into something more harmful. This is protocol at all levels, although baby Christians may not yet understand it.
- Step into childlike faith and trust God's plan despite what we see. This is kingdom high school protocol. Earlier levels struggle with this concept due to a lack of consistency.
- Learn to step into the come-up-here principle to see and understand God's plans. This is kingdom college protocol.
- When we make mistakes, get back up and start again. Fear of failure is not an option. This protocol begins in grade school and continues through our life journey.
- Learn to live an ascended lifestyle of living in Christ all day, every day. Like everything else, this takes practice. This is kingdom college protocol.
- Learn to act based on God's direction, not what head knowledge suggests. This protocol starts in kingdom high school. High school is about functioning outside of reasoning.
- When the Trinity gives an assignment, step into it despite fears, reasonings, feelings, personal desires, and emotions. This is kingdom college protocol.

- Be careful what we watch, listen to, time spent around, and what we read. Do these activities produce life or death? Avoid negativity. This is protocol for all levels.
- Check the ego at the door. An example of ego is "Look what God showed me!" In many cases, this isn't about witnessing to others. It's more about the warm fuzzies that we desire from others. This begins in kingdom middle school where our ego needs to be in check by the beginning stages of kingdom college if we plan to mature beyond a certain level.
- Watch our words! When we say things such as, "I'm sick today. My asthma is acting up. My arthritis hurts" and similar statements, we've owned the problem. The word "my" indicates ownership. Even the small words are powerful! When we learn to speak only what the Father says about us, we're functioning at the kingdom college level. Until then, we're in the K–12 grades.

We'll be at several K–12 levels in a variety of subjects at the same time. As we mature and step into the fullness of what kingdom college offers, we may spend a lot of time in the freshmen year establishing our foundations to make sure they are solid, just like I did. This includes ridding our minds of false paradigms and structures. How do we know what levels we're at? First, look at what causes negative triggers. Then, explore the thoughts behind the triggers. As you've seen through my examples, we can quickly take care of negativity. However, some of the consequences beckon us to engage in more kingdom training and paradigm shifting as part of the process of moving forward.

Emotional outbursts generally occur at the middle school level. All this indicates is that we need more healing in a specific area. It's no big deal unless we can't see the triggers. I didn't at first, so I asked to be quickened each time I was negatively triggered. Be careful if you request this! You might not like what you see. Another indication of stunted growth is when the same type of situation recurs repeatedly. We walk through a variety of healing and trainings in all levels of maturity, even into kingdom college. Dealing with our junk is a lifelong process, so even when we think we've arrived, we still have more work to do.

I'm extremely transparent in my stories. I'm not perfect nor do I think I have all the answers. I'm on the same path as you. If I can offer one piece of advice, it's this: When negative triggers come your way, address them immediately. This includes any unforgiveness, a key factor in the ability to move forward. We often don't even realize we haven't forgiven someone until it's revealed to us. Unforgiveness and any form of fear stop us in our tracks. I rejoice when I deal with fear because it's one step closer to another level of maturity. Learn to see the glass as half-full. Usher negative thinking out the door. Be consistent and proactive in seeking the things of God over serving fleshly desires. Allow the Holy Spirit to take precedent over soulish ways. Live from the spirit, not the flesh. Most of all, enjoy the journey no matter where you are!

I leave you with one exercise that greatly helps me. In the accompanying workbook, I provide additional activations I made up for myself as practice. Just like I practice my musical instruments to improve my playing skills, I practice key concepts in my kingdom school journey.

For the first four years of my journey, I stepped into the mobile court daily. I do it now as needed. Some call this the mobile court and others call it the court of accusations. In the heavenly court system, the mobile court is the first level for dealing with our personal issues. I dealt with the accusations coming against me and my family line in this court. Please note this is not the place to take others to court without their knowledge. We can stand with them as an advocate. They do the work, and we assist.

Science now says the 97 percent junk DNA carries the memory of our ancestral line. [7] They call it "epigenetics." Many say that genetics isn't really a thing because it's more about the epigenetics. That means our system carries the memory of previous generations in our DNA. Think of all the good, the bad, and the ugly that come with that. This is why I repent for my entire generational line when accepting charges.

Each morning, I stepped into the mobile court using the eyes of my heart—my imagination. I visualized standing in front of the judge and said something like, "What are the charges against me?" The Accuser was in the witness stand. Jesus was at my side and the Father at the judge's table. I'd stand as the Accuser spouted off a list of nasty stuff. I'd write all of it in my

---

7   Stephen S. Hall, "Hidden Treasures in Junk DNA," *Scientific American*, October 1, 2012, https://www.scientificamerican.com/article/hidden-treasures-in-junk-dna.

journal. When he finished, Father asked, "Do you accept the charges?" I always agreed. Had I not done it, someone in my family line did, and their actions affected all of us.

Next, I'd own the charges, repent for them, and renounce all ties. From there, I nailed them to the cross and covered them with the blood of Jesus. Lastly, I traded the accusations for more of God's character attributes, such as love, peace, joy, and kindness. I never wanted to leave an empty house. I journaled everything so that if an accusation came up again, all I had to do was go back to court and hold the Accuser in contempt of court. That never fared well for the Accuser.

I did this exercise daily for several years, eventually noticing that certain negative triggers no longer had the same effect on me. My attitude and circumstances slowly changed as I focused on building relationship with the Trinity, letting go of negativity, and practicing kingdom principles. Our behavior, paradigm structure, and daily habits clue us in to our level of maturity. When I'm not happy with what I see, I spend time with the Trinity, asking them to show me where I need to make adjustments. This key point can't be left out: rejoice in the small victories. Progress happens one step at a time. When we fall, get back up, get back on the path, and keep moving. I can't stress that enough. We can't let mistakes stop us in our tracks. Be prepared to make a bunch of them and learn in the process. Most of all, enjoy the journey from a position of rest and peace.

Lastly, I encourage you to read the additional chapters in *Maturing as a Mystic: Workbook* that I've not yet suggested. I take you through the process of discovering the purpose of your personal "temple of the Holy Spirit." I also introduce you to the seven spirits of God, the cloud of witnesses, and the four chambers of the heart. At the end of each chapter, I include activations for you to modify to fit your own needs as you step into the "come up here" principle. May you enjoy the journey!

Resources:

THE RESOURCES LIST includes groups, individuals, and organizations that provide opportunities to be interactive with others. It all depends on your personal style and what works for you. However, everyone needs fellowship. I'm no longer part of "organized religion." I left because I was called out of it and am now part of NW Ekklesia, a fellowship that functions as a team and isn't single leader based.

If you feel that some healing is needed, there are resources for that as well. If none of the suggested organizations work for you, then ask God to reveal his plan. Maybe He's got something else up his sleeve and simply wants you to spend time with him while he reveals it to you!

- **The accompanying workbook** – titled *Maturing as a Mystic: Workbook*. It can be found on Amazon. In it, I provide all the activations I practiced on my journey. I provide a PDF version on the Healing Frequencies Music and Supernatural Lessons websites. (See below for links)
- **Healing Frequencies Music** – https://healingfrequenciesmusic.com This is my music website where all my materials can be purchased. This includes PDF copies of all my books, music, and personal music (personal songs, sound baths, and Song of the Month subscription). The music is specifically created out of my interaction with the Trinity

as I learn to live the come-up-here principle. In addition, I have a YouTube channel where more music is available to listen to for free: https://www.youtube.com/channel/UCJY7TH_cgiIYSxMH71el83g

- **Supernatural Lessons** – https://supernaturallessons.com This is my "spiritual" website where I put up all my teachings that are related to maturing as Sons of God. For people new in this protocol, this is a great place to start. Most of the materials on this website were created in the first few years of my journey.

- **NW Ekklesia** – https://nwekklesia.com I'm part of the governing "council" for Northwest Ekklesia. We are all about helping people on their Kingdom School journey! There's a monthly subscription that allows people to participate in weekly online gatherings. Subscriptions include special teachings only for subscribers. We also have classes on various topics by those within the ekklesia. We are not single leader based and function as a council where everyone participates in various aspects of leadership. My teachings are available on this site as well.

- **Kingdom Equipping Center** – https://kingdomequippingcenter.com/ Gil and Adena Hodges began this organization. If everything you're reading in this book is new to you, this should be one of your first resources. They have interactive classes where you ask questions, do little assignments, and become a community. They have a variety of offerings so be sure to check them out. Monthly fees are reasonable where they have a variety of levels to choose from.

- **Engaging God** – https://eg.freedomarc.org/ Mike Parsons (from the UK) began this program to help bring people into Kingdom College as they learn to function in the come-up-here principle. It is entirely self-paced where you work alone through a variety of modules. Mike is a teacher, so the materials are presented in a progressive manner. Go as fast or slow as you desire. Monthly fees are reasonable. If your subscription stays active, you have access to the videos, downloads, and PDF versions of the videos.

- **Sapphire Leadership Group** – https://theslg.com/ This organization is led by Arthur Burk. If you need inner healing, this is one place to go. Arthur presents information that's in Kingdom High School but is essential for being successful in Kingdom College. If you need paradigm shifts in religious thinking, you'll get some of that here!

- **WOW Life Church** – https://www.wowmediaproductions.com/wowlifepodcast/ Kirby de Lanerolle and his wife, Fiona, are the senior leaders of WOW Life. He's quite a bit off the grid in Christian thinking where he brings an eastern perspective into the mix. He's from Sri Lanka and doesn't think like the western world. He also has a YouTube channel where you can listen to many of the services for free. If you want the socks blown off any religious thinking, this is a good place to go. WARNING: His teachings aren't for the fainthearted.

- **Son of Thunder Ministries** – https://www.sonofthunder.org/ is Ian Clayton's website. Like Kirby de Lanerolle, Ian's teachings are out-of-the-box. They will challenge all religious thinking so if this isn't something you're not prepared for, wait until you're ready. You can purchase individual teachings, conference sets, and bundles. They are all downloadable as MP3 files.

- **Ohel Moed** – https://www.moed-ministries.com/home Grant and Sam Mahoney run this organization. If you're in need of inner healing, this is one place to go. You'll be matched with someone trained in their methods based on your specific needs. They also offer mentoring.

- **Marketplace Ministries** – https://www.marketplaceministries.co.uk/meet-the-team.html Lindy Strong runs this ministry with the help of Bonita Curtis and Kay Reynolds. They have a wonderful program that assists participants in a variety of healing protocols – physically, emotionally, and spiritually.

ABOUT THE AUTHOR

Del Hungerford

D EL HUNGERFORD CURRENTLY teaches clarinet and music
education courses at the collegiate level. As a classical musician,
she uses her training to delve deeper into how frequency affects our
spirit, soul, and body. Connecting the spiritual with the material, Del creates
spontaneous prophetic instrumental music with the intent of physical, emotional, and spiritual healing. As an author, she writes about her experiences
in a format that's meant to assist others on similar journeys. Her recording
label *(and website)* is Healing Frequencies Music where she also blogs about her
research. She explores the spiritual side of that research through the website,
Supernatural Lessons.

Del holds degrees in music from the University of Idaho (B.M.), Yale
University (M.M.) and the University of Washington (D.M.A.). She's active as
a music educator in the Pacific Northwest and currently lives in north Idaho.
She's also a mentor and member of the administrative bench for NW Ekklesia.

www.ingramcontent.com/pod-product-compliance
Lightning Source LLC
Chambersburg PA
CBHW071624040426
42452CB00009B/1471